WHAT, ON EARTH, AM I DOING?

WHAT, ON EARTH, AM I DOING?

LIFE LESSONS ON LIVING

MADISON PRICE

KINGDOM KEYS
PRESS

Kingdom Keys Press

ISBNs: 979-8-9927783-1-1 (paperback)
979-8-9927783-0-4 (hardcover)
979-8-9927783-2-8 (ebook)

Cover and book design by Mayfly book design

Library of Congress Catalog Number: 2025904082
First Printing: 2025

For those who have enriched my journeys –
may you find a piece of yourself within these pages.

CONTENTS

INTRODUCTION

"What on Earth . . . ?"

We have all heard this questioning phrase uttered on numerous occasions, such as, "What on Earth are you talking about?" or "What on Earth is going on?" It is not uncommon for this expression to be heard in moments of exacerbation or even accompanying moments of shock or surprise.

In this book, though, I am going to challenge you to ponder the question, "What on Earth?" from a more introspective mindset. To dig deep and ask yourself tough questions about life, purpose, struggles, and loss. Essentially, to meditate upon the same question I have over and over throughout my life, "What on Earth am I doing?"

But do not worry. We are going to have fun on this journey. We are going to laugh along the way. We are going to realize together that sometimes it is easy to answer this question and other times it seems flat impossible. So, rest assured, you are not alone on this quest, nor is your life the one that is going to be examined under the lens.

Before we begin exploring this question, though, I want to clarify this is not your traditional story. Instead, the book encompasses a compilation of blogs I wrote over the last nine years woven into a five-part publication. Each part of the book focuses on a particular topic with the blogs grouped thematically as opposed to chronologically.

The hope is that by presenting the blogs in this format, with added commentary throughout, it enables me to enrich the messages of faith, hope, love, and laughter I aim for my writing to convey.

As you read, you will also notice there are QR codes at the end of each part. I firmly believe a picture is worth a thousand words, so as an added bonus, these QR codes will direct you to additional pictures associated with select blogs in the book. Alternatively, you may visit the website listed in my author biography on the back cover and navigate to the photos tab to view the images. This will enable you to gain a glimpse into the places and people described within.

We are now ready to begin our journey. And as we do, I encourage you to embrace how these blogs might challenge your current views or shift your perspectives on previously held beliefs.

If I am able to accomplish even just one of these aims, I will deem my mission of asking the question, "What on Earth am I doing?" a success.

PART 1

LIVING ADVENTUROUSLY

"Life is meant for spectacular adventures. Let your feet wander, your eyes marvel, and your soul ignite."

—Unknown

LIFE LESSONS LEARNED ONE
ADVENTURE AT A TIME

I believe it pertinent to start by explaining that I first ventured into blogging when I was in my freshman year of college. Though this is typically one of the more exciting times in one's life, it ended up being a difficult year for me as I attempted to adjust to unfamiliar surroundings. Writing subsequently became my therapy and has stayed my therapy to this day.

As I began blogging, I soon realized that my writing had the power to be therapeutic for others as well. I found many individuals were struggling with similar issues and my blogs were a way for them to process their troubles alongside mine.

One way I devised my writing early on to empower others was by using my blogs as an avenue to take individuals on adventures. Since I am an avid traveler at heart, I thought why not share what I was experiencing on each of my trips with my friends and family. That way they would have the opportunity to vicariously visit the same places and gain similar insights.

Therefore, in this first chapter, you will read about five of the adventures that have touched my heart the most because of the places I traveled and the lessons I learned along the way. Some lessons were readily learned while others required a bit more acceptance. Nonetheless, I hope you will allow yourself to be transported to each of these locations as we journey together to Colorado, California, Honduras, and Chicago.

———

We Lost the Parents (January 2019)

Normally I am not one to have New Year's resolutions, but I was challenged this year. My mom told me not long ago she missed reading my blogs, and she wanted me to start writing again. Her challenge: Write one blog post every month. I waited until the 27th of January, but hey I made it.

The issue has not been that I do not enjoy writing, just that I did not think I have had too much going on in my life that was worth writing home about. Since graduating, I have just been working and trying to adult as best I can. But though I have thought my life has been pretty uneventful the past six months, I realize if you look for the little things in each day, then there is plenty to learn from and write about.

Let us take yesterday for instance. I had the pleasure of driving to Dillon, Colorado to explore the ice castles. Now is this something I would normally enjoy doing? No, not really. I am cold 24/7, so placing myself in a situation where I would be even colder is just not my idea of a good time. I mean no offense Elsa, but the cold actually bothers the rest of us. But alas, I sucked it up and went because I had a strange feeling I needed to.

By the time I got to Dillon, the thermometer read 11 degrees, I had already encountered snow, and it was going on 9:00 p.m. I had to give myself a pep talk just to get out of the car.

But boy am I glad I did. The ice architecture was out of this world and the whole place had a majestic feel . . . well at least to what was left of me to feel. Five minutes in there and my hands and feet were numb. I am not even sure at this point that full circulation has been restored. But though my physical body may have been cold, my spiritual body was glowing.

As I walked around the ice features, I was amazed at all the different formations and how the lighting seemed to bring the ice to

life. At one point, I walked into a little cave and instantly became breathless. Dangling not five feet above my head were thousands of icicles as sharp as tacks. It was at that moment I understood the true beauty surrounding me . . . as well as the reason I had to sign a waiver before entering. I was literally one ice puncture away from death, but I would not have had it any other way.

As it grew later and subsequently colder, I started cursing myself a little for getting the tickets for a late time. However, I booked the tickets to the ice castles for later in the evening because I thought that would mean there would be less kids. That was not the case. The place was swarming with them, and for those of you who really know me, you know my mantra is, "No kids, no pets, no plants." The "no kids" is first for a reason. But you will be proud that I put on my best attitude of tolerance and braced the day care zoo. I actually have to admit, I delighted in the joy I was watching the children around me experience in the castles.

But there was one kid in particular that made me stop and really evaluate why I was there. I was walking around in the enclosure when these two kids appeared out of nowhere. One kid started looking around and then simply stated, "Whelp, we lost the parents." There was no panic in his voice, just blunt honesty. One thing I do love about children is their give-it-to-you-straight attitude. Honestly, though, the kid could not have cared less.

Though I joined a couple of other strangers in laughing at the kid's utterance, I also could not help but think that was how I wanted to live my life that year. The kids had been so caught up in their curiosity, they had quite literally lost track of their parents. But yet, they were not afraid to adventure and explore new things. In other words, their curiosity guided them more than their fear.

In that moment, I realized I had kind of lost that. I was fearless when I had studied abroad the year before and took every opportunity to explore. But I had come back and started living a complacent life again. I had fallen back into routine. So I decided right there I was going to reawaken my adventurous self to remember what it felt like to feel truly alive and full of curiosity. Thus, I joined the kids in sliding down ice slides and crawling through ice tunnels because at the heart of it, our adventurous selves are child-like. Sometimes we do quite literally have to lose the parents, or the cautious side of ourselves, to embrace the adventure that awaits when we allow ourselves to explore.

So, while my mom challenged me to the resolution of writing one blog post a month, I do not think that task is enough. Instead, I am challenging myself to living life one adventure to the next, so I ensure I always have something to write home about. I would encourage you all to do the same.

California Adventure (April 2019)

In February, my parents invited my sister Chandler, my brother-in-law Tanner, and me to go with them to California. My parents had to go there for a work convention and thought it would be fun if we tagged along. Since we all agreed a break from work would do us good, we booked our tickets to join them.

My parents ended up flying out over the weekend to get settled in with the plan that we would fly out late Tuesday night. On Tuesday of that week, Tanner and Channy picked me up at my apartment and then we drove to the airport. Now, despite how many times we told Tanner we were going to be really early, he simply did not want to listen. He insisted we would be cutting it close with turning in the rental car and getting through security.

The result: We were about an hour and a half early to our gate. Even more comical was the fact that our plane was about an hour and half late getting in. When we saw it finally pull up, Tanner innocently asked if we had to wait for people to get off before we got on. "Unless you want to sit on their laps, then yes," I could not help but answer. I really should not give him such a hard time; he has not flown much. I am also pretty sure he had no patience left by that point.

But herein lies the first lesson of this adventure. And men, if you take no other lesson away from this blog post, take this one: The women are always right. Period. And if you will agree to that, then it will save you your patience and possibly your sanity in the long run.

While we were waiting, I was taking a survey of the other passengers sitting in the airport, contemplating who my seat buddies might be. You see I was seat 23B, so I knew I was going to be sitting smack in the middle between two people. Just which two people I did not know. Most times it turns out to be screaming babies or unruly toddlers because God knows how much I love children. I did hear a couple screaming candidates in the waiting area, so I started praying and practically begging God to spare me just this one time.

Right as we began to board the flight, we looked over in the waiting area and watched a young girl throw up all over. Oh goodie I thought, the only thing better than sitting next to a screaming kid would be to sit next to a sick kid. Once we boarded though, I was relieved to find that I was going to be sitting between two adults, and better yet, no children were in sight. Shortly after breathing a sigh of relief, I got a text from my sister sitting three rows behind me. She had puke child sitting right behind her and a screaming child in front of her. I will tell you that was one moment I was glad I was not Chandler. "Enjoy your flight," was all I could respond as I chuckled to myself. "Oh and you might want to check your hair when we land," I could not help but add.

Unfortunately, our plane was even further delayed in leaving. We had just started to taxi when the captain came over the radio saying there was a mechanical issue with the auto brake and they needed to reset it. Sounded like a good idea. After sitting there for 20 minutes praying we would not have to get off and board another plane, the captain came on and said we had the all clear and could leave. At this point, though, we were over two hours late leaving. But the captain said not to worry; we would only be about an hour behind because we would make up time in the air. All I could think to myself was, "Do not push it too much buddy, because if you get us going too fast and that auto brake decides to malfunction again, all we can hope for is an act of God to stop this bird."

But luckily the flight proceeded without incident. Well almost. We were so close. Fifteen minutes before touching down, we started our descent and a child on the plane started screaming bloody murder. The child right behind Chandler. It never fails.

After listening to that for 15 minutes, everyone was ready to get off that plane. By the time we exited the airport, it was already going on 10 p.m. My dad had arranged for a shuttle bus to pick us up at LAX and drive us to the hotel in Anaheim, which when we routed it, our GPS told us it would take about 40-50 minutes. When the shuttle bus finally arrived at the airport, though, we discovered we were not alone on our journey despite the late hour we were traveling. That was when we realized we might be in for a really long night. Just how long we never could have guessed.

As we drove through California, it was evident the guy sitting in front of us had been having an even worse day than us. They had cancelled his flight in Guatemala the day before, so he had slept in the airport. Then when he finally arrived in Denver, they had lost his luggage. Luckily, he had a pretty good attitude about it, as he had us laughing the entire drive. The lesson I learned there was even when you think you are having a bad day, someone is always having a worse one. So learn to let go and laugh about the things that do not go as planned.

Like the shuttle ride that night. I am pretty sure if it would have been light and I looked out the window, I would have seen the Oregon border. I mean to tell you we drove all over California. There seemed to be no rhyme or reason to the route we were taking. We were even dropping some people off at their own homes.

At one point we decided to GPS where we were and were delighted to see we were only 17 minutes away from the hotel. But that did not last long. As the driver started to take the next person in the shuttle to their destination, we saw we were driving in the opposite direction that we needed to go. Our seventeen-minute arrival time turned into 40 minutes. That was when we unfortunately learned the driver had a list of passengers and had to drop them off according to the order on the list. That meant that what should have been a forty-minute commute from the airport turned into a two-hour commute because we were the last on the list.

We finally pulled up to the hotel at 12:30 a.m. and practically sleepwalked our way to our room. As I was taking a shower at one in the morning, I had an inkling Chandler and Tanner wanted to kill me for making them take such a late flight that night given that they are usually in bed by 9 p.m.

But the next few days in California made up for it as we all had a blast. We went to Disneyland, California Adventure Park, and Universal Studios, making the most of our time by riding as many rides as we could. My favorite of course were the roller coasters and adventure rides, though I know some of my entourage were not fans of those. What I thought was a little kid screaming in terror on one of the roller coasters ended up being my brother-in-law and my mom would not talk to me while we were standing in line to ride the drop tower because she was so scared. Honestly how I ever got her to stand in that line in the first place is beyond me. And if she was ready to hurt me before the ride, I know she was ready to kill me after. That one made us all scream.

Another thing we had to contend with on the trip was less than ideal weather. While we had numerous run-ins with rain, one night in particular was really fun. It so happened on that day, we were walking through Disneyland and stumbled upon a music parade with all of the Disney characters. I do not know how, but we ended up getting front row seats on the street to the show.

As we were standing there watching it, a light drizzle began. It gradually started raining a little harder throughout the parade, but still not enough to be a huge issue. In fact, when the parade was over, that little bit of rain had caused some of the lines to the rides to shorten. Therefore, we took advantage of this and hopped on a boat to ride through "It's a Small World After All." You know, the ride that repeats the same line over and over 1,241 times. But when we turned the last corner in that ride, a very different phrase came to my mind.

As the outside came back into view, all I could see was a torrential downpour of rain. "It's about to be a wet world" was my instant first thought. Unfortunately, there was absolutely nothing we could do to get out of the rain as we were stuck on the ride waiting for our boat's turn to unload. The lady running the ride thought she was funny by first thanking us for riding and then letting us know (in case we did not), it had started raining since we had entered the ride. You do not say.

The real problem with this downpour though, was that we could not find a taxi outside of Disneyland when we exited. That meant we had a 15-minute walk back to our hotel in the pouring rain. I knew we would be a sorry sight to see when we got back, but again the bluntness of children never ceases to amuse me. As we walked into the lobby of our hotel, a little girl turned to her mom and made the comment, "Eww mom, look. They are wet, like dripping wet." Great observation kid. I am pretty sure it took us all an hour to warm up after that rainy walk, and by morning our shoes were still soaking wet.

But I have to say, the weather never once deterred us from our plans. Neither did the fact that Disneyland seemed to be having mechanical difficulties while we were there. The castle was closed because it was under repair, the Pirates of the Caribbean ride that Chandler really wanted to ride was not operational, and even the roller coaster in Adventure Land was closed for the first few hours we were in the park. That about made Chandler and me hang it all up and go home. Disneyland simply just seemed to be broken.

The running joke with our family actually became that we were breaking Disneyland. It honestly seemed like every time we arrived at a ride, it malfunctioned in some way. For example, right when we got ready to board the roller coaster in Adventure Land, it quit working again. Then we were in line to ride the Goofy roller coaster and it quit working. Next, we tried our luck at the Peter Pan ride. Everything seemed to be going alright until we got in line and Peter Pan decided to stop flying. At that point, it honestly was getting comical.

But hands down the funniest moment was when we decided to ride the monorail around the park. The conductor had just come over the PA system to let us know at our next stop there was an amphitheater where a Disney show had just started. Therefore, if we got off the train, we could pretty much catch the start of the show. But right as the station came into view, we noticed there seemed to be some type of malfunction on stage. All of a sudden there was a little fire and everyone was being instructed to quickly exit the theater. Now it solely may have been a coincidence, but the fact we were passing the theater at that exact moment made us all bust out laughing as we were convinced our presence was cursing Disneyland.

But despite all the mishaps we faced along the way, the trip would not have been nearly as memorable without them. Nor would I have continued to learn so many lessons as I journey through this adventure we call life.

Our shuttle ride taught me that sometimes in life we experience detours, and we are not always going to be able to take the shortest route to our destination. If that is the case, then make sure you pay attention because you are on that alternate route for a reason. Search for its purpose and enjoy the view along the way.

The weather taught me we should never let the rain ruin our parade. Keep singing and dancing come rain or shine. And if it rains, no scratch that, if it pours, never let that stop you from getting to your final destination. Yes, you might arrive wet, cold, and unsightly, but what counts is that you weathered the storms of life and came out stronger on the other side.

And finally, broken Disneyland taught me that even the happiest place on Earth has its problems. So do not be so hard on yourself when things in life seem broken or beyond repair because you never know when a fix is just around the corner. Peter Pan started flying again, and so will you.

Honduran Adventure (July 2021)

I read a quote a while back that said, "That risk you are afraid to take may just be the risk that changes your life."

This summer I found there is much truth in that quote. In June, I had the opportunity to travel to Honduras and volunteer at the Holy Family Surgery Center on the Nuestros Pequenos Hermanos (NPH) Ranch. This surgery center is funded by One World Surgery and has three operating rooms, seven clinic/overnight bays, a dental clinic, and an eye clinic. But if you think this surgery center is like anything we have in the United States, you would be mistaken. That false assumption is for both good and bad reasons, which I will get into a little bit later.

But first I want to start with why this was a risk I was initially afraid to take. To be clear, traveling alone does not scare me, especially after living and traveling abroad on my own in the past. But my downfall with this trip was doing a little bit too much research before I went. When I booked my flights, I had to book flights that flew into and out of Tegucigalpa, which frankly I had never heard of before. I should have left it at that. But no, I went to Google and typed in the airport and immediately began to question if this trip was actually a good idea. It is worth looking up for yourself, but if you do not have the time, I will tell you really all you need to know. Essentially, this airport is considered the 2nd most dangerous in the world to land at because of the mountainous terrain and its very short runway. Google has some reassuring images of planes sliding off the runway just in case you were wondering. So armed with this new knowledge, I began to question if this was really the hill, mountain, or runaway that I wanted to die on. As I pondered that question, I kept reflecting back on the fact that when I am older, I want to be able to look back on my life and say, "Wow, that was an adventure" not "Wow, I sure felt safe." So, with that, I booked the tickets and asked everyone to start praying.

Clearly prayers were heard as I have returned safely; but that landing certainly was not for the faint of heart. It feels like a normal flight until the last five minutes when all of a sudden the plane takes a sharp 45-degree turn, drops in between two mountains, flies over houses close enough to see what is on the breakfast table, and hits the runway and the brakes at approximately the same time. The cross winds also were kicking up the day I flew in, so we came in rocking side to side. I do not think anyone questioned why there were porter potties on the runway when we landed.

But thankfully the worst part was now over, and I was off on an adventure. Shortly after landing, I met up with the group of volunteers in the airport and could tell instantly we were going to have a great time together. We came from all over the United States including Oregon, Washington, Minnesota, Colorado, Idaho, Texas, and Pennsylvania. In our group of 13 were surgeons, nurses, anesthesiologists, medical assistants, college students, and general volunteers. Everyone was extremely kind and we all bonded instantly, especially with our first topic of conversation: "Boy, what a landing."

From the airport, we had about a one-hour ride from Tegucigalpa to the ranch. We had to be escorted by a security detail because of the instability in the region. Again, just things you do not tell your parents until after the trip.

As we were driving along, the poverty of the region was so prevalent in the housing and streets that were littered with trash. Yet this was backdropped against some of the most beautiful landscape of rolling hills and mountains I have ever seen. The juxtaposition was truly quite striking.

When we arrived at the ranch, I was also blown away by how nice our accommodations were compared to what I had seen driving in. We were staying in the beautiful Moscati Center that was situated around an open courtyard with hammocks and palm trees. The center can hold up to 100 individuals, though our group was much smaller. Each room contained four beds with a private shower and toilet and opened into the courtyard.

During our tour of the ranch over the next couple of days, we learned the total size of the ranch was about 2,000 acres and provided housing for over 200 children who did not have parents who could raise them. The children are allowed to live on the ranch until they are 18, and are provided with schooling opportunities as well as programs that allow their parents to visit them. There is also a special needs community on the ranch for children who need extra support and care.

As we toured the ranch, we were not really allowed to interact with the children because of COVID, but it was touching to witness and hear their shouts of joy and glee as they ran around and waved to us. We also got to attend one of their mass ceremonies and it was neat to hear them all worshipping in Spanish. On the ranch is also a farm that houses pigs, horses, cows, chickens, and goats. The size difference between the animals in the United States and Honduras was eye-opening as their animals are basically nothing but skin and bones. There certainly is a food shortage in the country that was evident everywhere you looked.

As my group began to settle into our new surroundings, we started feeling a little bit safer in the country . . . until we had our group orientation. It started strong with a warm welcome, but then devolved into a list of alarming things we were told not to be alarmed about. Our personal favorite was, "Do not be alarmed if you hear gunshots, the army is doing practice drills about 1,000 km away. Stray bullets should not be an issue though." All we could do was laugh after that orientation. We also learned we were not allowed to flush toilet paper because their sewage system could not handle it. That was a learning curve for everyone.

But if anything, that was one of the things I appreciated most about the trip. The fact that we were all learning and adapting together. I have always heard travel can be a brutality and I think that is very true. Especially when traveling alone, you are forced to trust strangers because there is no familiarity to cling to. But luckily during my stay down there, I had two of the best roommates I could have asked for who I knew were looking out for me. We shared many laughs, late night conversations, and probably far too many TMI stories about what we were experiencing down there. But that was the thing, we were all learning how to live and function in a foreign country together. It required vulnerability with each other to ease any discomfort we might be feeling and to build strong friendship foundations along the way.

The greatest part of acting as a team was required in the clinic. While the clinic was stocked rather impressively, there were limited resources when it came to medications and instruments needed for surgeries. While down there, I even ended up assisting on two gallbladder surgeries during which I navigated the laparoscopic camera while the surgeon cut the gallbladder out. Now, have I been trained to do that? Absolutely not. But when there is a shortage of personnel and the surgeries have to get done, you play the role you have to play.

During that week, we also learned how to navigate daily power outages during surgery, figure out workarounds when we ran out of pain or anesthesia medication, and overcome language barriers we faced with each of our patients. By the end of the week, I had played the role of surgical assistant, pill packer, OR cleaner, equipment sterilizer, administrative assistant, and hand holder. This led to me subsequently being awarded the "Most Willing to Fill Any Role" award at the end of the trip.

But I only received that award because of the lessons I learned from the people down there. There was not a single Honduran staff member who was not willing to do whatever job needed to be done as they strove to care for their fellow countrymen. It was inspiring and it ignited a passion in me to emulate their traits. I truly have never been immersed in a culture that cares so strongly for their people yet are so welcoming to foreigners. I made wonderful Honduran friends during my short stint down there who welcomed me with open arms from the first day. I even had to pinch myself a couple of times because I had the opportunity to work alongside and spend time outside of the clinic with a wonderful nurse who had worked with Mother Theresa. Listening to her stories was incredible and I was so humbled to be in her presence.

I was also so impressed by the patients we served. Some of those patients had been waiting over 15 years for surgery and/or waited over nine hours each day to be seen in the clinic. Yet never once did you hear them complain. If anything, they were just so grateful to have the chance to be evaluated. It was in stark contrast to what I am used to in the United States where patients are yelling at you if they are not seen by the doctor in a timely manner.

The Honduran patients are also so much tougher than what we are in the United States. For instance, I watched a seven-pound uterine fibroid be removed from one woman as well as a hernia be repaired that was the biggest the surgeon had ever seen in his career.

16

Yet not once did those patients ever complain of pain or express pity for their situation.

My time down there made me realize that global health truly is my calling. Not so much because of what I can do for others, but because of what I can learn from others around the world in the field of health. I am, therefore, now keeping track of what I learn from each country I visit. In Honduras, I learned you do not complain, and you simply do what needs to be done.

My week down there afforded me other opportunities outside of the clinic as well. This included karaoke nights and a bonfire with the locals complete with s'mores and a campfire sing-along. I also had the opportunity to explore the ranch on beautiful hikes both with groups and by myself. A couple of times I will admit I got caught in torrential downpours on my hikes. That led to me either having to make the choice of seeking shelter and risk getting barbecued by the lightning popping all around me, or sprinting back to the ranch and risk getting waterlogged by the sheer amount of rain coming down. But overall, the weather was fantastic and the scenery was gorgeous. At the end of the week, I was sad to say goodbye to such a beautiful and peaceful place, so instead I said until next time.

My journey home turned out to be more eventful than I would have liked, but I have to say I think I jinxed it. I had said I did not care what happened on my way back as long as it happened after I got back to the states. In hindsight, that was not the smartest thing to say. On my flight back from Tegucigalpa to Houston, we had to circle for a while because of torrential rainstorms. But not to worry, the pilot told us, we had plenty of fuel. That is reassuring, I thought. Cue to 20 minutes later, the pilot comes back on and announces we have to fly to Austin because we are running out of fuel. That is less reassuring, I thought.

When all was said and done, the original three-hour flight ended up being about eight hours and I missed my connecting flight by 15 minutes despite sprinting through the Houston airport like a madwoman. Luckily one of the surgeons from our trip had his car at the airport, so he treated those of us who missed our flights to dinner and then set us up with rooms at a BNB in some quaint neighborhood in Houston. Sometimes I just have to laugh at the situations I find myself in. It is certainly never a dull adventure when I travel.

The next day I caught an Uber to the airport and joked with my friends from the trip that if I did not make it, it was David that did it. But David turned out to be a very pleasant gentleman who loved the Eagles, Elton John, skiing and could not wait to have his knee surgery in July so he could get back to racquetball. Thus, I realized if I had not missed my flight, I would have missed meeting David and making yet one more friend on this journey.

After another lightning storm that grounded my plane, a maintenance issue with a plane door that would not arm, and a flat tire that did not get fixed because of said lightning storm, my plane finally got out of Houston two hours later and into Denver right before a hailstorm hit Colorado. Again, all I could do was laugh at my luck and wonder if maybe I was turning into a storm chaser.

Honestly, though, this trip was an adventure I will never forget as it taught me so many lessons along the way. The first lesson is that sometimes the greatest adventure is simply a conversation. Those I met and conversed with along the way afforded me many wonderful memories I will cherish forever.

Second, never listen to what others say, go see for yourself. We all have assumptions and opinions of what other countries are like from what we have been told, but you really do need to go see it for yourself. Only then can you truly appreciate and learn from a place and its culture. And it is ok if you feel afraid to do so. Shoot, I did at first. But just do not let that fear stop you. In other words, be afraid, but do it anyway. You will soon learn that your fears do not know your strength.

The third lesson I learned is whether it works out or it does not, you will be fine either way. Some of my trip went as planned, most did not. I survived nonetheless.

And last but not least, I learned you never really travel alone. The world is full of friends waiting to get to know you. So go out and find some new ones; it will be the best decision you ever make.

Therefore, if you see less of me in the coming years, know I have gone out to find more.

The Windy City Adventure (October 2022)

Though I initially considered writing about my relocation experience to Missouri in this post, what I ultimately decided I would share instead is my recent epic excursion to Chicago. It was more of an adventure than my move, so I hope reading about it will be an adventure for you.

I will start off by saying the trip was a kind of a spur of the moment decision. I have a wonderful friend who lives in Chicago and essentially decided to text her a list of the next few weekends I had free. When she got back to me, I compared our schedules and selected the date from there.

When the chosen Friday rolled around, I finished up my duties at work, threw some clothes in a backpack, and walked out the door five minutes later. While I pride myself on not being much of a planner these days, I do think in hindsight I should have dedicated more time to packing for this particular trip. Why you may ask? Well, it is because I ended up forgetting to bring one critical item with me when traveling to Chicago in the Fall. Namely, a COAT.

Also, it was not until I was rolling out of my driveway that Friday, that I had ever given thought to punching my friend's address into my GPS. Upon doing so, I discovered I had about a six and a half-hour drive ahead of me. "Oh boy," was my first thought, but "Alright," was my second. I turned on the tunes and I was off.

Now something that might be helpful to understand about me is when I drive for travel purposes, I do not always choose the most sensible route. I often choose the fastest. One day I might need to seriously rethink that plan.

You see it would have been easy for me to head east on 1-70 to

St. Louis, and then north through Illinois to Chicago. But do you think Maddy took that route? Absolutely not. I went north first and friends, this is where I will provide you a geographic lesson on Missouri. There is corn, 90 Baptist churches, and very little civilization up North.

As I was driving on supplemental road K that merged onto supplemental road W that forked off onto supplemental road NN, I was laughing thinking to myself, "I sure hope I do not break down on these less-than-ideal roads." I mean can you imagine calling AAA and trying to describe your location.

"Ya . . . um I'm somewhere off supplemental road XYZ in between the 25th and 26th corn fields you will pass."

Honestly, the vultures around me confirmed there were more dead than living things in the direction I was traveling. I literally burst out laughing when I came to one intersection in the road and my two options were Paris to the right or Mexico to the left. Seems about right I thought; I am traveling with no clear idea of where I might end up. I just as easily could have been driving to those countries. Also, you may have picked up by now that Missourians are not too creative when it comes to naming their towns. I rolled through Florida about 20 miles later.

By the grace of God, though, I made it out of the corn fields and onto a populated highway. I figured I was doing pretty good at this point. That was until I saw the sign indicating the next town I would be driving through.

It just so happened that the highway I was on was about to take me through Hannibal, MO. And that just so happened to be the ONE town in Missouri my mom asked me to avoid ever going to after watching a less than reassuring Dateline episode. Sorry mom. All I can say is from the highway, the town looked like it had real charm.

As I continued my drive through Illinois, I was starting to get excited about leaving the rural landscape and hitting the big city streets again. Oh ho ho, how naive I was. My first clue I might be in for more than I bargained for in Chicago was when my friend texted me, "Traffic here tonight is crazy."

"Ahh I should be alright still. I have had a lot of experience driving in downtown traffic. I did it all the time in Denver," I reassured myself.

But let me tell you, just like Dorothy learned Oz was nothing like Kansas, I learned Chicago was nothing like Denver . . . it was Denver on steroids. I am not going to lie, the second I saw the city streets come into view, I knew I had probably been better off with my vulture friends on the rural backroads of Missouri. And while I would like to say I was wrong thinking that, I ultimately was not. Driving in downtown Chicago was CRAZY.

In all truthfulness, it had never been my intention to drive downtown. Prior to leaving for my trip, I had purchased a parking permit for an underground garage a little outside of main downtown to avoid the crowds. But when I arrived in Chicago, all my best laid plans went flying out the window. I think while we all greatly appreciate modern technology and the wonders of GPS, we also recognize sometimes it just lets us down. And those times often come when we are counting on it the most. Like when trying to park in a foreign city. Essentially, my GPS instructed me to make a number of unnecessary turns that ultimately ended me up on one of the busiest streets downtown . . . far from where I ever needed to be. I instantly felt like I was in New York City with the bright lights, honking horns, crazy cab drivers, and swarms of people.

As I was trying to park, I ended up doing not one, not two, not three, but four laps around the same three city blocks. By the fourth time, it was more of a lap of shame. I discovered the problem was my parking garage was located underground and that was throwing my GPS off. So, every time it was instructing me to take a slight right turn at one intersection, what it actually should have been telling me was to go through the light and then take a slight right down the ramp to the parking garage. I essentially found my destination when I decided not to listen to my GPS.

Luckily, once I parked, I was able to easily locate the pedestrian walkway to exit the parking garage. Yet when I exited the garage, I still found myself significantly underground. That was despite having climbed multiple flights of stairs. As I stood there looking up at the sky and streets above me, my only thought was, "Chicago, we have a problem."

In that moment, though, I just had to laugh. I mean I am sure we have all had those times in our lives where we find ourselves about four levels lower than where we would like to be. In that moment, that was me figuratively and literally. That parking garage was kicking my butt. Parking garage: 2. Maddy: 0.

I eventually discovered I had to climb seven more flights of stairs. When I exited the final door, I found myself back among civilization. I took a deep breath of the cool Chicago air and was on my way.

As I walked downtown, I could not get over how lively the city was. It was nice to be among the city scene again. I had not realized how much I had been missing it! As I wandered around, I eventually met up with my friend and could tell we were going to be in for a fun weekend.

The next day we decided to do the architecture boat tour along the Chicago River. It was an amazing experience filled with incredible views and historical facts of the buildings in downtown Chicago. I could not get enough of the scenery. That tour is a must do if you ever find yourself there!

As we were getting ready to pull into our docking spot at the end of the tour, we noticed one of the drawbridges was being lifted up for a couple of sailboats to pass through. It was really neat to watch the whole process play out while on the water. However, what started out as an added boat tour experience, slowly morphed into a comedy show. One of the boats was clearly struggling with navigation and found itself "parked" in our docking spot. The captain nicely informed the boat over the loudspeaker that it needed to move. Seemed like a simple enough request one would think.

However, as the boat attempted to move, it started heading right

towards our river boat. Now there was no question about which boat would win in the event of a collision. Thankfully, I was on the winning boat. Yet before any collision occurred, our captain rather brashly yelled over the loudspeaker for the boat to move, followed by an exasperated, "What on Earth are you doing?"

"Navigating poorly," would have been an appropriate response in my opinion.

In the end, the sailboat managed to eke by our big boat and everyone on the tour was left with a good story to tell. As the incident was unfolding, though, I could not help but reflect on how often we find ourselves in one or both of those situations. I know in my own life, I have certainly been the big boat yelling at things to get out of my way. Yet at other times, I have been the sailboat doing everything in my power to avoid colliding with what seems to be barreling down on me in life. I think that while we all prefer to be the big boat directing the course, we all too easily can relate to the sailboat and that hopeless feeling of navigating aimlessly. I guess my takeaway lesson was I need to practice grace when I am the big boat and faith when I am the sailboat.

Though I could keep going on and on about my weekend in Chicago, I will not out of respect for the time you are already taking to read my post. What I will say is my friend crafted the perfect two-day Chicago itinerary that enabled me to experience the best of what Chicago has to offer. I got to go to the zoo, walk along waterfront beaches, explore Navy Pier, walk through beautiful parks, ride on trains and buses all around the city, and drink fresh apple cider at an Apple Festival that was in town for the weekend. I gorged myself on ethnic food and had the types of conversations that reset your heart and soul. All in all, it was the perfect way to spend a weekend with a dear friend.

I was extremely sad when Sunday rolled around and I had to leave. I told my friend I was confident I could find my way back to my car and that she did not need to walk back downtown with me. In hindsight, that was probably not my best idea.

I easily got back to the main intersection downtown that I needed to get to in order to find my garage. I had to laugh because there were signs posted all over not to block the intersection, and I can almost guarantee you that on at least one of my four laps on Friday, I had been guilty of just that. What a tourist.

Eventually, I found the general area of where my parking garage was. But now you will laugh . . . I could not figure out how to get back down to my car. I could see the entrance I had entered on the main road, but the problem was there was no pedestrian access that way. Though I wandered around for 20 minutes, I could not locate the pedestrian access to the garage. As it was starting to get late and I knew I had a long drive ahead of me, I decided to make an executive decision I encourage no one else to make. I ultimately waited for the traffic light to turn red and then I sprinted down the road into that garage before any cars could challenge me. I got a few sideways glances, but I was committed to my decision. Sometimes in life, you just have to forge your own path. The added perk of my approach too was that I knew exactly where my car was parked from that entrance. Who knows how long it would have taken me to locate it had I tried to enter from the pedestrian access point.

Since I was late starting back, I decided I would take the road more traveled. I thought it was probably smarter to travel west on the major highway systems to avoid driving on the rural Missouri roads in the dark. As I drove out of the city, I had full confidence I was going to crush the road trip back. How silly of me.

I mean, I started off strong. However, about three hours into my drive, I started getting hungry. No problem, I thought, I will snack on the Kind bar my friend graciously gave me for the trip home. Now normally I would not bore you with the exact type of Kind bar it was, but it is important to know for the story. It was a dark chocolate peanut butter bar.

Delicious? Yes.

The most practical type for a road trip? No.

You see, that Kind bar had been trapped in the slightly toasty environment of my backpack for hours. In other words, the chocolate had started to melt, so that bar was MESSY. I mean to tell you I had chocolate everywhere. All over my hands, all over my face, in my hair. EVERYWHERE.

But not to worry, I thought. I have a wet wipe in my backpack.

Now I can only surmise that my doomed direction mishap took place in the four seconds I was searching for that wet wipe. That was when I must have hit my phone and turned my GPS route off. The problem was, I did not realize it until I was about 20 more minutes down the road. For that period of time, I was assuming I was still on the right highway because my GPS was not directing me to take any exits or interchanges.

To this day, I still do not know what made me look up into my rearview mirror, but boy am I glad I did because I noticed two things.

One: I still had chocolate smeared across my upper lip. Two: I was traveling Southeast.

Now I do not know how many of you have or pay attention to the little direction readout signal in your rearview mirror, but I am telling you it can come in handy. Essentially, when I saw the little green SE, I thought, "Oh no." If you need help putting two and two together, or you need a geography lesson, here it is: Missouri is west of Illinois, not east.

As I glanced down, I noticed my GPS was turned off. Sure enough, when I turned it back on, the first directive I heard was, "In 15 miles make a U-turn."

All I could think was, "Gosh, I miss my Colorado mountains."

In Colorado, I always knew when I was heading west vs. east. Unfortunately, the corn fields of Illinois and Missouri are not helpful in providing a sense of direction.

That unintended side trip tacked on about 30 minutes to my already six and a half-hour drive. I ended up rolling back into Missouri around 11 p.m. Of course I was tired, but I was also incredibly grateful for the adventures and memorable mishaps that my first time in Chicago had to offer.

———

I decided to give Chicago another try about a year later for a work conference. From the story below, you will see that maybe Chicago and I should just admire each other from a distance . . .

———

Partaking in the Marathon (April 2023)

Oh Chicago. You and I will be mortal enemies, yet forever friends.

This last week I decided to take on the windy city for a second time. I would like to report I had fewer issues this time than last, but would it really be a Maddy adventure if that was the case? No, I think not.

My trip started with a 5:00 a.m. flight into the city on Sunday. There are not many perks to flying at that time, aside from basically having the city to yourself when you arrive. With the light traffic, I was able to get downtown to my hotel pretty smoothly. That is about where all the smoothness of this trip stopped.

Since I was traveling for a work conference, my hotel accommodations had already been arranged. When I arrived at the Allegro Royal Sonesta Hotel, the woman at the reception desk was kind enough to let me check-in early. That would have led to an interesting nine hours to kill if she had not.

The hotel itself was beautiful, with sprawling staircases and glass chandeliers that made you feel as though you had stepped onto the Titanic.

But then I opened the door to my individual room.

I had to laugh when the first thing I noticed was the stark contrast between the hall carpet and the room carpet. One was elegant, one was zebra striped. I will let you guess which was which. The room also had other charms like bright blue closets, a neon ironing board, and bright purple and green pedestals. You got to love the hidden charms in downtown Chicago.

Since the weather was not great at that time and I had only slept four hours the night before, I decided to take a quick nap. When I woke up, I checked my weather app and saw I had a small window of clear weather.

"Should I risk it?" I asked myself.

"Yeah," I mistakenly told myself.

You see, I decided to take my chances and walk to the convention center to check-in for the conference. I figured that way I could avoid the crowds the next day. The issue, though, was the conference center was about three and a half miles away. That was going to equate to over an hour walk. Since I had nothing else to do, I set off. I made it about half a mile to Michigan Avenue before the rain, wind, and regrets started rolling in.

To this day, I do not know how I made it to the convention center.

There were times the wind literally blew me sideways, and then there were times I found myself walking through sketchy railroad districts that I will fess up to now (sorry mom and dad).

When I finally arrived, I was wet, cold, and could not feel my hands or face.

After I checked-in and was given my materials for the week, I laughed as I was flipping through the program booklet and landed on the conference center and hotels information page. It listed hotels within walking distance . . . mine was not on there. But do you think I hailed a taxi or solicited an Uber for the journey back? Nope.

Ultimately, about the same amount of rain, but maybe less regrets (as the wind was now at my back) accompanied me on the walk home to my hotel. That night when I got back, I cranked the thermostat to 80 and left it there all week.

I am happy to report, though, the conference itself was amazing!! While I could write pages and pages about it, I will not out of respect for your time and probably your interest. What I will say is that over the course of the week, I attended over 40 education sessions, sat in countless exhibitor demonstrations, and listened to leading keynote speakers from all around the world. Given the conference was focused on health information technology and management systems, many of the conversations focused on artificial intelligence, machine learning, interoperability, and automation.

There were so many great educational sessions offered that I often found myself running from one building to the next to squeeze in as many as I could. This proved to be challenging at times given the convention center is the largest one in North America. I definitely got my steps in and fully understood why everyone calls HIMSS the marathon conference. Five days truly was an incredibly grueling duration for a conference, and I was certainly feeling it physically and mentally by the end. But I have to admit, I loved every minute of it.

Perhaps my favorite thing about the conference was the conversations I had. I am not an individual who enjoys networking events; in fact, I made it a point to not attend any while I was at the conference.

I wanted my conversations to occur naturally, not begin in a contrived location. Thus, I made it a point to have some of my greatest and deepest conversations on the shuttle bus to and from the convention center every day. This enabled more relaxed and comfortable dialogue and provided me the opportunity to converse with individuals from all around the world about their products.

I also had many wonderful conversations on the exhibition floors, but I have a sneaking suspicion that it was more because of the nature of my job than anything else. I had to laugh because the instant the exhibitors found out I was from a healthcare system, the red carpet was rolled out as I became their customer. If only they knew how little clout I actually have.

But I took full advantage of my customer status as it enabled me to sit through demos of their products and systems. And I will tell you, if artificial intelligence does not excite and scare the crap out of you at the same time, it should. I had the opportunity to interact with talking lamps that are aiding fall prevention, robots that are taking vital signs, and chatbots that could answer any question I asked. The technology was out of this world and took up three exhibition floors at the conference.

Not surprisingly, though, a lot of the conversations revolved around the ethical considerations of AI. In my opinion, these are very valid conversations. There is certainly no doubt health tech is our future given staffing shortages and the need for automation. But I do think as a society, we need to keep reminding ourselves that just because we can, does not always mean that we should. We still have a responsibility to safely serve our communities, and we need human connection to do so.

As I reflect back on the week, I realize there were so many times I felt like a fish out of water. I do not come from a strong health tech background, nor am I around it much in my day-to-day job. In fact, many asked why I would even choose to attend this type of conference over others offered for my role. My answer is because this past week forced me to stretch and challenge myself. Each night I had to go back to my hotel room and research terms and topics I had heard that day because I wanted to understand the conversations going on around me. Doing this ultimately allowed me to have conversations with vendors at the end of the week about topics that had been way over my head initially. For example, I started the week hearing about this thing called "fire". By the end, I understood what they were actually talking about was "FHIR". We all had a good laugh over that one.

The one thing I will never forget about my time at this conference, though, is what one of the vendors told me during a conversation. He said, "Maddy, never stop asking questions. Even if the answer is no now, it does not mean it will be no forever. It is going to take innovative minds and forward-thinkers to change our industry, so never stop doing your part. I respect the type of administrator you want to be because you are not only concerned with how to manage these systems, but you also desire to understand the science behind them. Never lose that. That is how you will gain the respect of everyone exhibiting here as you become an administrator."

As I walked away from that conversation, I could not help but think the reason this conference was so transformative for me was because it not only spoke to my administrator heart, but also my science heart. The conference was a perfect way to marry the two.

Now before I wrap up this post, I do not want you to think that Chicago was all work and no fun. There was no shortage of excitement on this trip as I got to attend a comedy show and rock concert, watch a police chase, and witness a seven-firetruck alarm response right outside my hotel.

And even the conference itself provided some excitement. Out of all the sessions going on at the time, I just so happened to be in the one session where the moderator passed out cold on the stage right in front of us. It was scary in the moment, but memorable and comical in the long run. I can only surmise that because I was the youngest individual in the room, I was the one chosen to run and get the AED machine about two flights of stairs down. Thankfully, the gentleman was ok, and we were able to have a good laugh about it afterwards. I mean, if you are going to pass out, you might as well do it at a health-care conference in front of an ER physician and prior cardiac medical assistant. The three of us now share a story and experience we will never forget.

I will say, as the convention ended, I was sad to leave. Chicago, though, was nice enough to provide me with one last piece of excitement. It came by way of my trip to the airport.

I thought I was leaving in plenty of time at 2:30 p.m. to get to the airport for my 5:30 p.m. flight. Friday traffic in Chicago taught me otherwise. The result was a nail-biting close call, with me arriving at the gate about five minutes prior to boarding. All I know is that if they say HIMSS is the marathon, my journey through the airport was the sprint.

But it is a sprint I would do again and again if it enabled me to learn and grow as much as I did that week.

———

As we wrap up this first part, I want to thank you all for adventuring with me to these places that touched my heart. If there is anything I have discovered over the last decade of my life, it is that life truly is best lived one adventure to the next. There are so many people to meet and cities to explore if we are willing to embrace both the good and bad we undoubtedly will encounter along the way. I hope through my writing, you were able to transport yourself into these environments, and experience both the highs and lows I did while I was there.

I also hope reading about these adventures demonstrated that in some of these places I understood what on Earth I was doing, while in others I did not. I think we all know which category Chicago falls under . . .

Nonetheless, whether I did or did not know, I never hesitated to embrace the adventures and life lessons learned along the way. Hopefully, you were able to resonate with some of the lessons that each location taught me as you read along as well. Or that you will be able to apply them to your life moving forward.

To close out this section, I would like to meditate, though, on the greatest lesson I have learned across all my adventures. And that is the truest and greatest adventure occurs when you are willing to throw all caution to the wind.

On each of these adventures I shared, no doubt there were times I was flat out scared. For example: on a plane ride to Tegucigalpa, on a ride down a drop tower in California, when taking my chances of getting punctured by an icicle in the ice castles, or when (poorly) navigating downtown Chicago.

But though I may have been frightened, I did not let that stop me from trudging on. Because while our comfort zones may be familiar and safe places, I can assure you nothing worthwhile grows there. We only grow when we are willing to push the limits of what makes us comfortable because only then do we become aware of what we are truly capable of.

So, as you plan your next adventure, I would encourage you to ask yourself, "Where would I go or what would I do if I was not afraid?"

Your greatest adventure is right on the other side of overcoming that fear. And who knows, it might even just be that one thing on Earth you were meant to do.

Scan to View Images

PART 2

LIVING ABROAD

"The great glory of travel, to me, is not just what I see that's new to me in countries visited, but that in almost every one of them, I change from an outsider looking in, to an insider looking out."

—Clara E. Laughlin

ESCAPE TO THE EMERALD ISLE

I f I contend that my adventures to the locations described in the previous part of this book touched my heart, then I must say the adventures I experienced while living abroad in Ireland touched my soul.

I was fortunate to have the opportunity to study abroad in Cork, Ireland for five months during my junior year of college. I had never been out of the country before, so I knew I was going to be in for quite the experience. What the full experience turned out to be . . . I never could have imagined.

While over there, I participated in an archaeology class that enabled me to travel all around the island and gain access to some of Ireland's most coveted landmarks. I also enrolled in multiple folklore classes and joined countless student organizations to enmesh myself deep within the Irish culture. I figured if I was going to take the leap and live abroad, I might as well embrace life as a local instead of as a tourist.

But honestly, my relocation to Ireland could not have come at a more pivotal moment in my life. I had recently lost my aunt, who was also one of my best friends, to a stroke less than a year before I moved. Therefore, I was struggling to find meaning in my life.

I will let you read, by way of the following blog posts, how Ireland was able to restore that meaning and so much more.

Getting Lost and Loving It (*August 2017*)

Thank you everyone for the well wishes for my travels! I have arrived in Cork and have started to get settled in. I cannot say the entire process has been smooth, but it certainly has been manageable. I was able to make both of my flights out here, and that is saying a lot because I am always late to virtually everything. Luckily, the flights were without incident. Upon landing in Cork, I picked up my luggage and hailed a taxi.

On the way to the apartment complex that is serving as my home for the semester, I started to experience some of the culture shock I was anticipating. The houses are so close together and there are electricity wires running all over the place. It made me realize I take a lot for granted back in the United States.

That was even more evident when I arrived at my accommodations. The complex was not quite what I was expecting, but since they have a housing shortage in Cork, I am just grateful to have a room. And honestly my room is pretty nice. It is just a little foreign to me that to flush the toilet you have to pull a lever on the wall. I also keep hearing comments from my roommates that the shower and kitchen are too small. I will admit I have found some interesting ways to contort my body to fit in the shower, but hey learning something new about yourself is always fun. I guess I could look at it as everything is "too small", but actually I'm beginning to think maybe in America everything is just "too big". The toilet, shower, and kitchen all do their jobs in Ireland, so maybe they are exactly the size they need to be.

Also, while they do have cars here, there is no way you would ever find me driving one. Two cars can barely fit side-by-side on the road, all of them are stick shift, and everyone drives on the opposite side of the street. Two minutes tops and I guarantee I would be in an accident.

Thus, I have resorted to walking. Over the last three days, I have

walked over 20,000 steps each day exploring the city. One day alone I made three trips to the grocery store because of how far I have to carry my groceries home.

But I have loved every minute of my walks. Today I walked around the city for five hours straight. I journeyed into countless shops, ate at local restaurants, shopped at the famous English Market, and found just about every pub in Cork on my quest to scope out the best one.

I have also explored my school grounds, and let me tell you, the university I am studying at is unreal. I swear I will be going to school in a castle. The grounds are incredible, and the architecture is out of this world. I do not start classes until Monday, but I can already tell I am going to love them. I get to travel all around Ireland and next week I am already making my way to Dublin. I am so excited for this journey to begin.

Most importantly, I am learning how to get comfortable with being lost all the time. I have always been the type of person who has to know in exactly what direction I am heading. That, though, has certainly not been an option while I have been here. I do not have access to the Internet on my phone, so I cannot GPS my way around.

Therefore, I have resorted to wandering aimlessly and letting adventure find me along the way. For example, today I found myself in some alleys I probably should not have been in, then at other times I found myself on the busiest streets in the city. I found a homemade gelato shop way out in the boondocks and then thirty minutes later happened to stumble upon a farmer's market where I sat and enjoyed some of the local music. And honestly while I truly have been lost at times, I do not want to ask for directions. It is not that the locals are not friendly and would not help, it is just I am loving seeing what all I find when I lose my way. It is like I get lost, but at the same time I find myself.

The one piece of advice my mom gave me before this trip was to make lemonade out of the lemons I would undoubtedly encounter. I have already run into some rather unfortunate circumstances, like my paper grocery bag ripping open on the streets and my groceries tumbling out. But I remembered my mom's advice and made the best of the situation. A local was even kind enough to help me out, so that day my lemonade was made a little bit sweeter.

I am discovering that adventure is out there, and I cannot wait to see where all it takes me in the next few months. I pray you are all healthy and well and I would appreciate your continuous prayers for my journey.

You Choose (*August 2017*)

I struggled this week to come up with a title for my blog post. I had several ideas in my mind for one, but my experiences this past week really just could not be defined by a single title. I have had great times, and I have had not so great times as I continue to navigate my way through this foreign land. Thus, what follows is 100% truthful. You cannot make this stuff up, even though sometimes my ego might have wished I could.

Option 1: Everything in Ireland is Cold and Wet Including Me

If any of you ever have the notion of visiting me, I beg you to please bring a jacket, umbrella, and ten layers of body warmers. And if you still have room in your suitcase, will you please bring the same for me? Why I came to Ireland without one heavy jacket, I do not know. What I do know is I am always freezing. The nights are cold, the mornings are cold, and 7:00 a.m. to 7:00 p.m. are cold. The sun might be shining on occasion, but even then, God is performing this new magic trick where the sun seems to be producing no heat.

More often than not, though, it is cloudy and rainy. It has rained every single day since I have been here. I have given up on my hair, I just embrace the frizz, and I virtually go nowhere without my rain jacket. At night, I sleep with three pairs of socks on while crouched in the fetal position. I am used to the dry cold in Colorado, but not this wet cold, and believe me there is a difference.

Now I do not mean to sound like Ireland is all doom and gloom. It is not. The buildings and countryside cast against the overcast sky create some of the best scenery I have ever experienced. And being cold all the time does have its advantages. They say your muscles burn more calories trying to warm your body, so I cannot complain too much about free workouts. I guess I just have to keep looking on the metaphorical bright side, because let's just face it, Ireland rarely has a physical one this time of year.

Option 2: Adulting is Hard Enough, Adulting in a Foreign Country is a Whole New Level

For the sake of being honest, I will just admit right here I have struggled this week with some basic adult life tasks. I always knew adulting was going to be a challenge for me, but man did I sure decide to take this challenge to a whole new dimension by studying abroad right after I reached my 20s. What can I say, I like a challenge.

It all started with opening a foreign bank account. I thought I would go in, sit down with a banker, and get it all set up. Well . . . I was wrong. They sat me by myself at a computer and told me I was going to do it online. Great.

I got to the first screen and knew this was going to be a guessing process. They asked me for my tax number . . . what? The kind assistant informed me that meant my social security number . . . so why did it not just say that? Oh now you want my CAO number . . . huh? Again, the kind assistant informed me this was my student ID number. That was obviously what I was thinking it was. Basically, the assistant was asked ten different questions in the span of 15 minutes and I still had to go back later to get further clarification on my account. The great news is the account is now open. The ironic news is there is not a cent pledged to it. I am killing this adulting thing.

While I was acting grown up, I thought I would go and register with immigration to become a resident. I was slightly terrified to do so because at orientation a lady had put the fear of God into us about this process. She told us not to argue or question the officers, and to stay very compliant because they could easily decide whether we stayed in their country or not.

So, I set out this morning with images of burly men in Kevlar vests smoking cigarettes and throwing people out of their country. I think I was so scared that I got lost along the way. Actually, that is not true. I got lost because I just keep getting lost. I have been in Ireland for ten days, and I have gotten lost ten days in a row now. I really need to invest in a good map and learn how to find my way like an "adult."

In case you were wondering, though, the immigration officer was one of the kindest ladies I have ever met, and we even exchanged some jokes with each other. If her Kevlar vest was under her wool sweater, I could not tell. And I am proud to say that I am now a resident of the Republic of Ireland.

While I was on a roll, I thought I would complete my final adulting duties for the day. That meant checking out the laundry facilities and taking out my trash. Laundry was up first. I responsibly entered the code for the laundry room, and upon entering, scoped out the washers and dryers. I was about to exit when I realized I was locked in. Now I am all for safety and appreciate that I can feel secure in the laundry room, but being locked in from the inside seemed slightly overkill. I spent five minutes investigating how to get out of the room before I found the exit button. Luckily, one push and freedom was granted.

Now you would think I would learn from my laundry experience about the increased safety measures this apartment complex has. Apparently not.

When I decided to take the trash out tonight, I again had to punch in a code to open a gate for the dumpsters. That was all fine until the gate closed behind me and locked. I did not panic, though, because I remembered how they like their exit buttons here. So, I responsibly found the exit button and pressed it. The only problem was that it was broken. I literally was locked in with the trash.

I was contemplating scaling the gate when an individual passed by. Wonderful! I kindly asked for help, and then heard the two worst words you can hear when you are locked behind a gate . . . "No comprendo." This woman clearly spoke Spanish and not English, and she looked at me in exactly the way I felt . . . like a crazy person locked in with the trash.

I did not panic though and somehow convinced her to come closer to the gate. I was trying to explain to her in my broken Spanish how to punch in the code on the keypad. I soon realized, though, I had a problem. The gate code was 0125. Now while three years of Spanish had taught me that one was uno, two was dos, and five was cinco, I for the life of me could not remember what zero was in that moment. Nunca? Nada? (Those are both wrong by the way.)

But by the grace of God, she got it, and I was set free for the second time in one day. I laughed all the way back to my apartment complex and decided I am staying away from locked mechanisms for a while. Apparently, even the simple adulting things are too hard for me.

Option 3: I Lost My Heart in a Pub

Since adulting has been a challenge, I was glad for the opportunity to be a student again and travel for my class these past few days. I stayed in a youth hostel in Meath and got to explore the countryside of Ireland. Two nights ago our professor took us to this pub, and I instantly fell in love. No, not with my Irish husband (though I am still looking), but with the culture and people of Ireland.

The pub had a live band that was phenomenal. There were about 25 of us that were American, and the rest were all Irish. The leader of the band would direct sing-offs between the Americans and the Irish with popular songs and then everyone in the pub would sing together.

We stayed at the pub until midnight and listened to music while enjoying drinks. I realized I could so easily become accustomed to this culture because the Irish celebrate each other and are so much more laid back in their way of life. Visiting that establishment was everything I had wanted my first pub experience in Ireland to be. I would love to be in that environment all the time because I know I would come to appreciate life and relationships so much more.

So, this post is titled "You Choose." Maybe you can sympathize with "always being cold" or you identify with the notion that "adulting is hard." Or maybe you know what it is like to "lose your heart" and achieve such genuine happiness like I did in a pub way out in Ireland's countryside.

I hope this blog, with its different titles, spoke to you in at least one way as it illustrates an imperfect person trying to navigate a foreign land and learning so much in the process. I know there is still much to discover during my time here. So onward and upward my friends to the next experience and lesson.

Learning From the Landscape (*September 2017*)

I have been involved in an archaeology class for the last three weeks that has taken me all around Ireland. Now, anyone who knows me might scratch their heads and say that makes no sense. They may say, "Your major is not archaeology," or "You do not study anything close to that at home," or even "The idea of your germophobic-self digging in dirt is really just beyond comprehension."

It is ok to admit you might have had these thoughts, because frankly I did too before I got here. But roaming the landscape of Ireland these last three weeks has truly changed my life.

I have to admit, I came to Ireland with a rather heavy heart. This last year has been extremely hard. When I lost my aunt, I lost one of my best friends. We had one of the closest relationships I have ever had in my life, so a part of me broke when she passed away unexpectedly. I have been trying to figure out who I am now that she is gone, and I have not been doing a very good job at that. So in a way, I came to Ireland to find myself and become the person who God wants me to be. Surprisingly, I have learned more about myself in the last three weeks than I have in the last 20 years. And most of this knowledge has come from observing the landscape of Ireland. Let me explain.

On one of our field trips this past week, my class encountered a cheveaux de frise. Do not even try to pronounce it . . . I gave up trying the first day. But basically, it is a thicket of sharp rocks that are stuck in the ground and point upwards. The cheveaux de frise is usually situated around a fort and was used for defensive purposes to slow down attackers so they could be picked off by archers. Now you could all probably care less about knowing that, but this simple feature caused me to reevaluate my life.

I have noticed over these past few months, I have been erecting these stones around my life, and more specifically around my heart. I have been so afraid of getting hurt or feeling more pain, that I have tried to guard my heart in a similar manner. But what I noticed in the landscape was that the most important feature of these cheveaux de frises (I bet your pronunciation is almost there) is they have an opening in the wall. This opening is what allows passage for the people who live in the forts as well as for welcome guests. If you did not have this passage, then your fort would become desolate, and you would be cut off from the world.

With that realization came the greater realization that I have been cutting my heart off for months now. I forgot about that critical passage and the need to let people in. I tried to defend my heart and my emotions by keeping them all inside, but my world was thus becoming a lonely place. So, I have started tearing down some of those pointy rocks and creating paths that lead to my heart again. I am committed to inviting more people in, even though I know this might bring me pain. But I think if my aunt were here, she would want me to love this life and everything in it so fiercely that no stone could ever hinder that love.

Speaking of stones, Ireland is full of them. There is even an Irish saying that states, "If God sends you down a stony path, may He give you strong shoes."

When I was climbing down from this hillfort on the Aran Islands the other day, I was on a really rocky path. You certainly had to be careful because one slip and you might turn into a human domino. On my way down, I came across this woman in her 70s who I could tell was having a tough time getting down. She looked a little panicked, so I walked over to her and started talking to her about the beauty of the island.

Thirty minutes later, I knew where she was born, how many kids she had, what she had done for a living, the highlights and lowlights of her life, and that I really liked her because she was very supportive of me finding an Irish husband. When we got to the bottom, she thanked me for keeping her mind occupied from focusing on the slippery climb

down. It struck me how a simple conversation can mean so much to someone. That had not been my intention, but God works in mysterious ways. Up on that mountain, I had asked Him to reopen my heart, and by the time I got down, both a path to my heart and a friendship had been forged.

I thought that since my rain boots were not good shoes at all for that stony path, I would come up with a different Irish saying. Mine is, "When God sends you down a stony path, may He give you good **company**." That lady was the best company I could have asked for.

After descending from the hillfort, my group had to get back from the Aran Islands to the mainland. That meant we had to take a 50-minute ride on what I called the ferry coaster. On the journey back, our boat encountered some of the biggest swells I have ever seen, and everyone's stomachs dropped about ten times during this trek. I mean to tell you, babies and grown men alike were screaming. Even my germophobic self was tempted to kiss the ground when we arrived safely on the other side.

But the swells of the sea taught me another valuable lesson. Namely, life is going to be rough at times. Or in other words, life is going to throw you around like a rag doll just like the sea did to that boat. There are going to be highs when you are riding that wave, and then there are going to be lows that result in that pit in your stomach. The important thing is to weather the storm and ride it out. The boat could have stopped in the ocean, but then we would have been sitting ducks in even more danger. Thus, I learned you have to go with the flow and push through the storms to emerge even stronger.

I have been weathering a storm for a while now, but I am slowly learning how to navigate it and embrace the highs and lows I experience. Plus, with God as my captain, my ship is in the best hands. So, my advice to myself, and to you, is to face that storm so you can arrive victorious on the other side.

Truly, over these last several weeks, I have discovered that travel brings power and love back into our lives. I am learning so much more about myself and who I am now. I am also learning how to love from the bottom of my heart again. I credit that to God, the courage my aunt gives me from above to face each day in a foreign land, and all your prayers and support.

Sending all my love and best wishes from Ireland.

————

To provide some context, this next blog post was written shortly after the mass shooting at the Route 91 Harvest music festival in Las Vegas in 2017.

————

Uncomfortable Yet? (*October 2017*)

I have been working on writing this blog post on and off over the last couple of days. Two days ago this blog had a much different meaning. Then again, two days ago everything was better than what it is today.

My original message was going to be to challenge each of you who feels "comfortable" in life to go out and find what makes you "uncomfortable." Seems silly now in hindsight. Unfortunately, the truth is we are living in a world that makes us feel more and more uneasy and scared every day.

For me though, the last two months of my life have been quite "uncomfortable." I have been living in a foreign country for over seven weeks now and there has never been a time that I have truly felt at ease. My surroundings are constantly changing, as I interact with new people and places every day. For instance, I have slept in more places in this timeframe than I have in the past two years of my life. Sometimes I am sleeping alone, sometimes I have found myself sleeping in a room with 20 other people, and sometimes I have found myself sleeping on a middle bunk bed with a female stranger below me and a male stranger above me who did not even speak my language.

The bottom line is that each hostel I have stayed at in Ireland has made me uncomfortable. I have even had to turn a blind eye to those mysterious stains on the pillows, mattresses, and linen as I do not want to even think about what they are or how they got there.

Sometimes the surroundings I have found myself in are charming, like the countryside hostel I stayed at in rural Ireland. And other times I am staring at purple and blue walls that have polka dotted toilets and wondering who was allowed to decorate the place. So yeah, they are not always places that I would willingly choose to stay.

But wait. I have willingly chosen to stay in those places. I have chosen to go on those trips and put myself in those situations. I have chosen to be uncomfortable.

And I am telling you if I had not chosen to be uncomfortable, then I would have missed out on a lot. I would have missed the opportunity to cross over a section of the Atlantic Ocean on a rope bridge. I would have missed the opportunity to cross the Giant's Causeway off my bucket list. I would have missed the opportunity to visit the peace walls in Belfast and leave my own message of love. Most importantly, I would have missed the opportunity to sing Christmas songs on October 1st at the top of my lungs in a tour bus filled with 45 individuals from countries all around the world. So yeah, I would have missed the

opportunity to live life a little richer these past few months if I was worried about feeling uncomfortable.

And I now find this notion of seeking a state of discomfort even more imperative. With everything going on in our country and around the world, we are becoming more and more afraid of feeling uncomfortable. We have this notion that achieving comfort in our daily lives will lead to a sense of safety as we can predict and schedule how our days are going to pan out.

But today proves that is not always the case. When tragedies like the Las Vegas shootings unfold, we attempt to recoil as much as possible into our safety corners and not come out. We seek comfort and we let our fear of the uncomfortable and unpredictable stop us from living the lives we could. Though I cannot even begin to understand why events like these shootings occur, one motive is usually to instill fear and intimidation. I encourage you to not let that keep you in your comfort corner.

Truthfully, if I have learned anything these past two months, it is you have to start doing everything that you once said, "There is no way I could/would do that." For example, I used to say I cannot go to a certain club's meeting at night because I have homework, and I do not know anybody who will be there. I decided that was not going to be an excuse anymore in Ireland. I went to that club meeting, I met new friends who I now spend time doing things with, and I never once thought about any homework I had. It is funny how all the things I once thought I could not do, have become the very things that are actually quite easy to do now. But the key is that you must take that step away from what you normally feel comfortable doing.

In all reality, this experience abroad has changed me. I used to be so uptight about my studies and planning each day down to the last detail. I would freak out if something did not match my expectations or God forbid, I found myself in uncomfortable situations.

Now? Now I hardly do any schoolwork, my days are as unplanned as they can get, and I find myself in uncomfortable situations all the time. I live a bit more recklessly, love life a lot harder, and spend a lot less time worrying about anything but the present.

And while some may think I have slipped into madness for the way I have changed, I think it would be madness to have experienced all I have and then come back and live the life I once did. As I have learned to adapt to the environment around me, it has made me appreciate more and want for less.

I always said my main goal was to come back from Ireland filthy rich. Rich in adventures, rich in knowledge, rich in experience, rich in laughter, rich in health, and rich in love. That wealth only starts accumulating outside of my comfort zone, so I am losing no time living each day as uncomfortably as I can. I hope you will join me in doing the same.

Why Did You Choose Ireland? (*October 2017*)

Why Ireland?

I cannot begin to tell you the countless times I have been asked this question. Both before I came to Ireland and every day since I arrived.

I sincerely do not mind people's curiosity, but I always feel like I let them down a little bit when I can never supply a satisfying answer. I usually respond with, "I heard that all of the people are really friendly," or "They say it is absolutely beautiful there." You know . . . the cookie cutter answers.

I guess the truth is that for the longest time I did not know why I chose Ireland myself. Maybe I still do not know even though I have been here for over two months.

But I can tell you at least two reasons why I did not choose Ireland:

1. **To work on my tan.** First off, this albino does not tan, but even if I did, Ireland would have been the wrong country to come to. I am pretty sure I have seen the sun ten out of the 64 days I have been here. And while I have been to many beaches in Ireland, do not be fooled. You do not see beach towels and folding chairs with Coronas in hand. You see people with scarves, beanies, rain jackets, and waterproof boots at every Irish beach. Those who are brave enough to venture into the water only do so in wetsuits, and you can still hear that scream of initial shock when that first wave of ice-cold water hits. So yeah, I am not coming home with tan lines, but even better yet, I am not coming home with burn lines.

2. **To experience a predictable climate.** I also did not choose Ireland for its predictable weather. Coming from Colorado, I am used to bipolar weather. We see that one day it can be 90 degrees outside and then the next it is snowing. But while I always thought Colorado's weather was crazy, Ireland's weather is bipolar cranked up by ten. You can go through four seasons in shortly under one hour. For instance, the other day I was walking down the street in the heat of the sun (Summer), then the wind picked up rustling orange leaves out of the tree (Fall). Soon, clouds set in, the sun disappeared, and the wind

had a bite to it (Winter). Then, out of nowhere the clouds gently separated and a fine shower of rain began (Spring). Oh and that all happened in the time span of seven minutes and 43 seconds. I timed it. So, I can definitively say I did not choose Ireland for its predictable climate.

Why then did I choose Ireland? Maybe that why was answered this past weekend.

On a whim of a decision, I decided this last weekend to pack my backpack and travel five hours to meet two local strangers in their 60s in a foreign town near Galway.

When I arrived in Connemara, Sara and Charlie took me to lunch, and in an instant, I knew I had just made two great friends. The conversation flowed easily, and they too were fully supportive of me finding a young Irishman to marry. In essence, they were my kind of people.

When we arrived at their house later that day, they showed me to my private room and shower. It was the first time I had that kind of a luxury in Ireland, so I could have cried. Charlie then took me on a walk along a beach five minutes from their doorstep. Of course I was outfitted in gloves, earmuffs, a scarf, rain jacket, and rain boots (you know, standard Irish beach wear) as we strolled along. I watched their dog play on the shore against the backdrop of mountains and islands beyond the rolling sea. It was picturesque.

Over the course of the next few days, my "weekend with the locals" got better and better. Sara taught me how to cook and bake some of the most delicious recipes as she let me help her in the kitchen. She was also my personal tour guide as we drove through the windy roads of Connemara passing by abbeys, harbors, and bays. She took me to a wool museum so I could learn how they spun wool for their famous Irish sweaters, and of course we did some local shopping. We also took a long drive out to an almost deserted part of the island and got live lobsters from a local fisherman to cook for dinner. What an experience that was.

(If you are squeamish you might want to glance over this next part. Frankly, I am not even sure how the germaphobe in me overcame this feat.)

I think the daunting nature of the lobster feast really hit me when I sat down and there were two beady eyes staring at me. This was not going to be Red Lobster where the tail came nicely presented with the meat fully accessible. No, I was going to have to crack and dig. At that point, I think I just dissociated my brain from the task at hand.

First question I was asked was do you want a male or female?

"Oh, it does not matter," I casually responded.

Male . . . you want a male anytime you are asked that question. But since I did not know that, I received a female and spent the next five minutes peeling bright red lobster eggs from her underside. Honestly, I just forced myself not to think about it. Then off came the head and claws and out came some green and black stuff I just pretended not to see. As I began to peel away some of that discolored gunk, all I could think was my mom's care package that was coming with my disposable gloves was arriving just a little too late. I could have used them that night, but I just plunged on.

When it came time to crack the shell, I knew I was in for a challenge when Sara and Charlie kept saying they were the toughest shells they had ever handled. I mostly needed help and relied on them for the cracking. Using my little meat digger, I finally got the tail meat out.

I think at this point with lobster juice on my hands, clothes, and probably in my hair, my face must have conveyed everything I was feeling inside. Sara quickly offered to pour water over my lobster tail to further wash it while I held it over the sink, and Charlie got me a new plate because mine was filled with lobster gut juices, eggs, and who knows what else. I was so out of my comfort zone, but have no fear, I trudged on. I was determined to eat as the locals do.

I think that night I ended up eating more lobster eggs than I care to admit. I tried to just not think about it as I moved onto the claws and continued cracking and digging for meat. I took a hot shower after the meal and decided it is well worth the money to pay Red Lobster to do all the work for me. At least then my hands would be clean.

The next day Charlie took me on an hour hike in the Connemara National Park; the views were incredible. We also hardly got rained on, so I could not complain. After our hike, we shared a scone and drank tea in the little cafe and continued sharing stories. I learned quite a bit about Ireland in that cafe. Charlie then taught me how to make the famous Irish brown bread when we were back at the house. I thought that might be my last local food experience on this trip. I was wrong.

That afternoon, one of Sara's friends phoned and asked if they would like to come to dinner. When Sara said they had a friend staying with them (me), her friend invited me along. It was funny when we got there because her friend and her husband thought I was going to be one of Sara's friends, i.e. about 40 years older than I was. They were both quite surprised when a 20-year-old came bee-bopping out of the car.

While dinner was still cooking, we sat around the fire and enjoyed glasses of wine. Alan, one of the hosts, just kept pouring glass after glass for me. After three, I started to feel it. We finally made it to the table around 8 p.m., and trust me, I tried walking as straight as I could on my way there. I learned the meal was local lamb that had literally come from 50 feet away from their front door. Even though I do not eat red meat, I decided I was just going to embrace the local cuisine and give it a try. Alan started carving up the lamb, but not before he poured me another glass of wine. If you are keeping track (which I clearly was not at the time) that is now four glasses.

But now looking back, I am grateful for that 4th glass of wine that made me less than sober because when Alan cut into the lamb, blood came out. I am pretty sure if I had fully been with it, I would have gotten up from that table and left. But in my hazy state, I ate the lamb, blood and all, which most likely by that time had soaked into my potatoes and vegetables. I then washed it down with (yep you guessed

it) my fifth glass of wine. The walk up the steep stairs to my room that night was fun to say the least.

I think I was almost on the verge of learning "Why Ireland?" while staying with Charlie and Sara, but I needed just one more day. Or I needed just one more glorious hot shower. After all, those are rare in Ireland. I got my wish.

I was getting ready to pack late Sunday night when we got a call that all bus transportation was going to be shut down the next day. Tropical storm (ex-hurricane) Ophelia was about to make landfall on Ireland.

The next day all of Ireland was literally shut down, and so Sara and Charlie were kind enough to shelter me for one more day to keep me safe. The wind was never bad where we were, but we did get a lot of rain. It was the perfect excuse to stay in the house by the fire and watch movies all afternoon. I also learned to bake and cook some more. That rare hurricane in Ireland was my blessing in disguise. It helped me finally answer, "Why Ireland?"

So, am I in Ireland to try new things? To meet new people? To experience new joys and overcome fears? I am learning maybe all of the above. I got to sample the local cuisine (though not sure I could do it again), I got to share stories and laughs with two locals who are now great friends, and I got to continue to explore the Irish landscape while learning so much about myself and Ireland in the process.

So maybe I did not choose Ireland, but Ireland was chosen for me. Maybe Ireland was chosen to push me out of my comfort zone, to force me to try new things and meet new people, and to open my heart along the way. I started this weekend with only email contact between two strangers almost 40 years older than myself. I ended the weekend with stories and memories 40 years cannot erase.

Thus, I left Connemara with two new blessings in my life, and who knows how many more I will leave Ireland with when my time is up.

We Put the FUN in DysFUNctional (*November 2017*)

Life in Ireland got a little sweeter this past week with the arrival of my family. I will not lie that in a place where I have not seen a familiar face from the past 20 years of my life, it was nice to finally see my people. But notice I said life got sweeter, not that it got easier or more functional. I think that in even just one week, my parents and sister came to understand why I am functioning at best at a sub-optimal level in Ireland. In other words, Ireland is not without its challenges, even for them.

Before I met up with my family, I was sitting in class and got a text from my sister that read, "We already took a wrong turn and got lost going from the airport to the hotel."

Naturally, this would be an understandable statement when you consider they were trying to navigate in a foreign country, except for the fact that the hotel was literally a two-minute drive from the airport. Worse, you could see the hotel from the airport terminal. I think that might have been the first time I really knew talking my dad into renting a car might not have been my best idea.

The next text that came in 30 minutes later read, "Do you have any idea how we turn on the lights in the room?"

And I thought I was struggling in Ireland. I think what my family learned really quickly (and what I had been trying to tell them all along) is Ireland operates very differently from the United States. Things are not as straightforward as one might assume. It turned out you had to stick your key into a special card slot and then turn on the light switch. Ireland is all about saving energy.

As my lecture was wrapping up, I knew my family would be on their way to meet me. I had a split-second fear that maybe I should have taken a bus to meet them because if they got lost coming to me, we had no way to communicate without Wi-Fi. But, by the grace of God, we found each other in a parking lot in Cork where we embraced in the biggest hugs. We were all on cloud nine.

After a quick tour of my school and current stomping grounds, I led the way into the city for dinner. Since it was my mom's birthday, and I know her reluctance to stray far from familiar food, I had reserved a table at a Mexican restaurant. I know . . . what a great Irish tradition I was giving them. Couple that with the fact that the waitress barely understood any English, and the meal slowly morphed into confusion. My poor family probably thought they were in Mexico not Ireland.

Then of course, as if scripted by God Himself, the most traditional Mexican band began to play in the restaurant. In my defense, my parents had wanted to hear traditional music while they were here. They never specified it had to be Irish. And of course, to my dad, it did not matter. He started singing along and as embarrassing as it might have been, I can honestly say I had missed him so much that I welcomed the sound of his "beautiful" singing voice in the crowded restaurant.

The next day we decided to explore Ireland by car. Now when convincing my parents that they really did need a car to see Ireland, I might have left out a few details about the driving here. I had warned my dad about the tiny size of the roads and that he would be driving on the opposite side than he was used to. But what I might have left out was the fact that Ireland loves their roundabouts. My dad . . . not so much. We could not help but bust out laughing when the GPS led us through about seven roundabouts in a row.

It became a ritual for my dad to verbalize his driving actions every time we entered a roundabout to ensure we took the right exit. Although maybe we needed a different strategy, because as often as I heard my dad direct himself, I heard the GPS direct itself to "recalculate." In other words, we took as many wrong turns as we did right. For some reason, my dad also loved to accelerate either right before we entered the roundabout or right as we entered the roundabout. Then other times he would just stop after he entered one for no reason. As you can imagine, this made for some interesting encounters. We almost got smashed by a van in one and we could have rolled down our window and kissed the bumper of a tour bus in another. Thus over the course of the week, we learned how to dodge cars and buses while listening to some elicited expletives from my dad as in "Oh shit we have a bus!" Believe me, there was no shortage of laughter, prayers, and screams heard in that car.

And while just driving in Ireland was difficult enough, the GPS did not help. I am pretty sure by the end of the trip, my sister, Chandler, who was serving as our navigator, was about to smash it. You see, the GPS was great for getting us to where we needed to go, but for some unknown reason, it seemed to prefer roads in Ireland that could barely fit our car. Half the time we would be driving along a main road, only for the GPS to make us turn on some back road that was not ideal to drive on. Then, it would have us return to the main road five minutes later. The back road served no purpose except to increase the level of stress experienced in our car.

You may think that we would have learned to ignore the GPS's terrible suggestions, but no, we continued to follow those ill-advised instructions. We were worried the one time we did not, we would pay the price by actually missing some important turn. Believe me, we never did. But we certainly got a tour of rural Ireland as we constantly traversed those back roads.

The other problem with driving on the back roads in Ireland is that besides the narrow roads, the hedges grow right up against the side of the road. So, while you are trying to avoid smashing into cars on one side, you are also trying to avoid smashing into hedges and stone walls on the other. Chandler was just waiting for the side mirrors to go flying off. Funny enough, even the rental car lady was impressed when my dad returned the car with the side mirrors unscathed. Or as she put it, "It is impressive that the car's 'side wings' are still intact."

Clearly that is a problem for the returned rental cars in Ireland. Not surprising.

Besides the little driving mishaps we encountered, we did manage to make it to most of our destinations, though not always without incident.

For my parents' anniversary, I decided to take them on a boat tour to the Aran Islands and along the Cliffs of Moher. The issue was that we had to drive about three hours in order to get to the pier for a ferry that left at 10:00 a.m. that morning. That meant we had to be up at 5:00 a.m. to leave the hotel by 6:00 a.m. Somehow, we managed to do that, and after a few wrong turns in the dark, we were on our way. Of course, the GPS directed us along a back road where we soon met a long line of traffic. We saw that everyone was flipping around because apparently a truck was blocking the road. Since it was now going on 9:20 a.m., we were starting to sweat a little. We flipped around as well, but soon lost the line of cars we were following. We were flying through the countryside with no sense of direction and a deadline to make.

As we were driving along, we happened to pass by a little school where I saw a woman in the schoolyard. I told my dad to pull over so I could talk to her. Now I would like to believe I do not look like a threatening individual, but the way she corralled the kids into one corner of the schoolyard with a slightly panicked look on her face, told me maybe I should work on my approach. I think the stress of getting to the ferry might have been showing just a little too much.

But after she learned it was only directions I was after, she happily pointed us in the right direction. As we sped along, we were not sure if we would end up back on the same road that was blocked.

About five minutes later, we saw flashing lights and thought we were done for. We discovered there was a huge truck jack-knifed in the road, completely blocking the cars. But the little side road we were on was just past the point of this truck, so we were literally able to squeeze by and be on our way. It could not have been any closer.

But if there is one thing I love about Ireland, it is the fact that nobody is ever on time. After such an eventful morning, we laughed pretty hard at the fact that we actually made it to the ferry early and were the first in line. Only in Ireland.

The tour itself was magical. The boat ride along the base of the Cliffs of Moher might have been the best thing I have ever seen in Ireland and maybe even my life. I also took my family to my favorite spot on the Aran Islands.

In order to get to the top of this spot, there is a little hike. It is that stony path I told you about before. This path proved challenging for my mom and provided humor for the rest of us. I will admit the rocks are slippery, but not as impossible to climb as my mom made it look. Chandler and I laughed the whole way up as my dad practically dragged my mom up the hill.

While on the island, we also took a bus tour with a local tour guide. We all found the tour fascinating, or so I thought, until I turned around and found Chandler fast asleep in the bus.

But Chandler falling asleep had been a theme for a couple days now on the trip. She fell asleep in my room the first night they got here, she fell asleep countless times in the car when we were driving places (not the best for navigation), she fell asleep on the boat ride to the islands, and now here again she was asleep in the back of the bus. Poor thing was flat tired. We kept giving her a hard time about it.

There was one time, though, when our guide spotted seals in the ocean and slammed on his brakes that about made Chandler pay for her napping. As the van came to a sudden and abrupt stop, Chandler was jolted from her sleep and about thrown off the seat onto the ground. I was not sure my mom was going to be able to stop laughing.

But after a couple of days in Ireland, we learned the trick to keeping Chandler awake – pump her full of coffee in the morning. Coffee in the morning could make Chandler last all day.

In fact, every time you pumped coffee into any of my family, it was amazing how alive and spunky they became. A cup of coffee in hand and my dad started singing every song on the radio in the car. I do not drink coffee, but I have a nagging suspicion that Ireland must put something a little extra in theirs . . .

Of course, I would not let Chandler (the coffee queen) come to Ireland without trying the true Irish coffee. She ultimately did not like the strong Whiskey taste, and neither did my mom. My dad and me? We enjoyed the drink and the burn that accompanied it on the way down.

Speaking of liquor, I could not allow my family to come to Ireland without going to a pub. We tried a few in the city, but they were a little too busy for a family affair. We finally found a quaint one that had a live Irish band in Cork. We decided to share a bottle of wine to commemorate the night.

After my experience a couple weeks ago, I decided it was best to pour my own glass and keep it to a minimum. My dad, however, got a little carried away when pouring my mom's glass. Halfway through our meal, my mom announced she was a little out of it. Her one large glass of wine was making her feel funny. It was quite evident she never drinks and now I think I know where I get my alcohol tolerance from. But the pub turned out to be a great success with great music, great food, and even greater conversation. A true Irish experience.

But if there is one phrase that summed this entire week up, it might just be, "It seemed like a good idea at the time."

I will leave you with one more of our adventures.

We decided one day to go shopping in the small town of Skibbereen. We were enjoying looking through the small shops at the local craftsmanship when we stumbled upon a long line of people. A very long line of people. I mean a line that extended for blocks and blocks and wrapped around street corners.

Naturally as any good tourists would be, we were very curious to discover what this long line of people was for. We decided to walk on the other side of the street and follow the line to see where it led. Some of us were betting it was the opening of a new restaurant. Some thought maybe it was a new movie or play that was showing in town. It was even hypothesized it was a line for a popular church service. As we continued to walk along the street and see the line getting longer and longer, our curiosity kept growing.

Now before you read any further, I would like you to take a guess as to what the line might have been for. Ok have you made one? Props to you if you get it right because the cause of this line never crossed our minds.

So, like I said, we were continuing down the road and becoming more and more excited to see what the fuss was all about. All four of us learned the source of this line at about the same time. As we passed by the building all of the people were entering, we read the sign above –Skibbereen Funeral Home. At about that same time we bumped into the hearse parked on the side of the road.

Now there is nothing funny about someone dying, but thank the Lord there was a store to our immediate left that we could duck into (or pretend we were headed to all along) because we were hysterical. The thought never once crossed our minds we would be following a funeral home viewing line. But I am telling you what, whoever had passed away must have been very important and influential in that town because I am pretty sure we saw the town's entire population on the road that day. Looking back now, the fact most people were dressed in black should have been a tip off. But like I said, following the line just seemed like a good idea at the time.

In all honesty, the week I spent with my family in Ireland was better than I could have ever imagined it would be. I was so content to finally have a piece of home around me again. Every time I am around my family, I am reminded of how blessed I am to have the best family

in the world. My sister is hands down one of my best friends, and my parents are the two best people I have ever known. They are generous beyond measure. I always feel a little unworthy around them because there is nothing I could ever give them that would in any way come close to what they give me on a daily basis. Their life talks, wisdom, and advice are second to none and they love with everything they have.

The laughs and memories we shared on this trip will remain in my heart forever and Ireland will always be extra special to me because I got to experience it with my people.

————

The following two blogs are not set exclusively in Ireland, but did take place while I was living abroad. I share them as these trips throughout Europe further touched my soul and taught me important life lessons that ended up radically shaping the way I now live my life.

————

Plan B (*November 2017*)

Have you ever had what you thought was a solid plan end up completely falling apart? I mean one that implodes so much you cannot help but laugh about how confident you had once been in said plan? Well, if you have, you can empathize with me. And if you have not, well then, you can learn from me.

This week Plan A had been to travel to Amsterdam, Belgium, and Paris over the weekend and stay in Europe until Tuesday. The fact I am writing this blog post from my apartment in Cork on Sunday tells you that plan did not quite pan out.

Not to bore you too much with the details, but I think I really knew this planned trip was a bust when I woke up Wednesday morning and had an email asking me to rate my hotel experience in Belgium. Well, I thought, I would love to, except I did not actually have an experience to rate. This thought ran through my head as I was laying in my bed in Ireland that morning.

I had booked my hotel room for the wrong weekend and clearly missed my check-in date. So, without a place to stay for a few nights, I was thinking I would just be better off staying at home on the Emerald Isle for the upcoming weekend. But being so close to mainland Europe, I just could not pass up the opportunity to go experience it.

So that is when I switched to Plan B. Plan B was virtually having no plan at all. Instead, I decided I was just going to buy a plane ticket to Europe for the next day and quite literally fly by the seat of my pants.

When the next day rolled around, I woke up at 3:00 a.m. and got a taxi to the airport in Cork. Once I arrived in Amsterdam, I took a train to the city center, locked my backpack in the luggage locker, and set off to explore the city on my own.

Not too long into my journey, I quickly learned that mainland Europe is not Ireland. As I was walking along, I noticed most of the shops were high end fashion boutiques; I had yet to see any number of those in Ireland. Amsterdam also does live up to its stereotype of the place in Europe for marijuana and prostitution. The city was brimming with it.

Not to worry though, I did not choose to participate in either one. I did have to laugh one time when I saw a sign for a store advertising one thing and clearly selling something else. I remember how when I innocently entered this store to buy souvenirs, I was hit smack in the face with a thick cloud of marijuana smoke. As I glanced around, I had a sneaking suspicion their "homemade baked goods" in the glass counter near the register had a little something extra in them.

I will not lie, though, I was a little shocked at the sexual culture of the city. But rest assured, even though I did walk along the Red Light District for a brief second, I never feared that I would be at risk for human trafficking. "Why?" you may ask. Well, it is because I am always cold.

As I walked down the district that day, I had on boots, four layers of clothing, a scarf, ear muffs, gloves, and the hood on my jacket was up. With little of my body actually exposed, I left a lot to the imagination, so much so that men did not even bother to look my way. And whether their lack of interest in putting me in the market was due to the fact that I was the most unfashionable person in the most fashionable city, or because I looked like a nun on my way to the abbey, I did not care as it made me feel all the safer.

But Amsterdam was not all that bad as I embraced the idea that when in the Netherlands, you have to experience the Dutch way of life. And I did experience it.

My trip was full of everything Dutch, including windmills, wooden clog shoes, tulips, and bicycles. I went into countless museums, and I even got to go to the Anne Frank house. My favorite part, by far, was the food. I devoured Dutch pancakes with syrup and powdered sugar, and while I do not often eat cheese, I gorged myself on cheese on my trip. I went to the Cheese Museum and honestly, I think I spent two hours there. I tried every cheese in that shop with no shame. I had lavender cheese, smoked Gouda cheese, coconut cheese, pesto cheese, cumin cheese, honey cheese, herb cheese, fresh cheese, aged cheese, cow, goat, and sheep cheese. One more hour in there and I might have become lactose intolerant. But it was all delicious, and if I had been flying home from there, I would have packed my bag full of cheese.

As the day wound down, I considered doing a canal cruise to see the bridges lit up at night. However, I also knew I needed to catch a train to get to the city of Delft where I would be staying for the evening. Therefore, I ducked into a Dunkin' Donuts because they had the strongest Wi-Fi signal around that I could use to check the train times. That strong Wi-Fi connection revealed a horrifying truth to me. The train I needed to be on left in 30 minutes.

Now you might not think that is a big deal, but it was. First off, I was about 20 minutes away from the train station, and I had yet to buy a ticket or get my bag out of the luggage holding area. Couple that with the fact I was alone and in the dark with no GPS. That meant I was going to have to run directionless through a foreign city. It likely comes then as no surprise that I thought this feat might be too much for me this time.

As I took off, I felt like Forrest Gump, except I was running blind, and just praying I was headed in the right direction. By the grace of God, I saw the train station and literally sprinted the rest of the way. I bought my train ticket and probably looked like a criminal stealing luggage with how fast I was in and out of the locker area. I ran to the information desk to find where my train left from (I had no clue how to function in a train station) and sprinted up the escalator and onto the landing platform. I jumped onto the train at 5:37 p.m. and had to ask people around me if I was even on the right train. I probably should have done that before I got on, because no sooner had the question formed on my lips, than the train sounded its whistle, and I was off. But luckily it was the right train, and though I had to stand in the area between cars for most of the journey, I was excited about what Dutch adventures the next city would bring.

I arrived in Delft around an hour later and met up with my cousin Jessica. It was of course pouring rain on our walk home, but Ireland had taught me to just embrace the precipitation at that point. Once we arrived at her house, I was able to get settled in my room and take a glorious hot shower after a delicious meal.

The next day was by far my favorite. I rode bikes with my cousin and her three kids all around the town of Delft and got to see churches, pottery stores, windmills, and yes, sample even more cheese.

Jessica and I then decided to take an adults-only bike ride through the countryside. The views were absolutely breathtaking, and the company was even better. I had missed being on a bike so much and loved the opportunity to get out in nature. While my bike did not have brakes (which made for some rather interesting situations on steep hills), I never once felt the desire to slow down. Ultimately what that bike ride taught me was that maybe I should just embrace abandoning caution and going full steam ahead at times in life. In other words, stop planning so much, and instead, do what I had that weekend and just go.

Before I left Delft the next day, I spent time wandering through the lovely little town on my own. I visited with local shopkeepers, and we talked about life and how we had each gotten to where we were at that moment. Some shopkeepers were even kind enough to show me their favorite inventory in the stores. And while I could not talk to some because I do not speak Dutch, I found that if I was not afraid to ask if they spoke English, I could have some deep and meaningful conversations.

I ended up leaving Delft around 7:00 a.m. the next morning, and since it was still mostly dark out, I had the whole marketplace to myself. It was one of the most serene moments as the sky had a slight orange tint that cast the church in a beautiful silhouette. I absolutely loved being able to experience that scenery as I walked to the train station that morning.

When I arrived back in Amsterdam, I took a very relaxing cruise through the city canals to conclude my European weekend. I then made my way to the train station to buy my ticket.

While I would like to say I was able to walk to the station this time, alas, I cannot because I was in desperate need of a bathroom.

So again, there I was running through the streets of Amsterdam like a madwoman in search of a facility.

As I skidded into the train station, I could not help but laugh as this is where mainland Europe compared to Ireland again just boggled my mind.

In Ireland, any pub, restaurant, hotel, or shop lets you use their facilities for free. Heck, if you leave some better than you found them, they might even send you out with a complimentary pint. But in Amsterdam? In Amsterdam, I had to pay to use the bathroom in the train station. Do you know how hard it is to find coins and think logically about all the steps you need to perform to put the coins in the machine when really all you can think about is your need to go to the bathroom?

But rest assured, I avoided an accident, and all was well again.

Though most of my return trip was unplanned, I was able to make it to the airport with plenty of time to spare. That turned out to be a good thing because I ended up walking the entire airport just trying to identify my check-in location. As I boarded the plane, I quickly understood why I had gotten my last-minute return ticket for 15 euros. It appeared as though a child had constructed the plane out of Legos, with seats as thin as paper.

Luckily the plane did not deconstruct in flight, and I was able to arrive safely back in Dublin. I had a four-hour bus journey back to Cork ahead of me, and as fate would have it, two kids at the back of the bus decided to have a screaming contest for most of it. I just had to laugh at my life where one day I am riding a bike along a peaceful river with low conversational tones, and then the next I am sitting in a crowded bus with children screaming at the top of their lungs. I guess life is all about balance.

Since sleep was not an option for most of that ride, I did a lot of reflecting. I reflected that in the span of three days, I rode on two planes, four trains, one taxi, one bus, one boat, and one bike. My legs carried me over 60,000 steps as I traversed two cities, and I met and talked with countless people along the way. And to think that I almost did not give myself the chance to go.

So my advice to you is when Plan A does not work out, do not be tempted to scratch the whole thing. Move on to Plan B, or better yet, do not plan at all and just go.

The Final Journey (December 2017)

I cannot believe my time abroad is coming to an end. I have absolutely had the time of my life and would not trade this experience for anything. I have learned so much that could never be taught in a classroom, and each day has been an adventure. At times, my life has seemed like a fairy-tale, and at others, it has been a complete mess. I have succeeded and I have failed in the past five and a half months, but I am discovering there is a lesson to be learned no matter the outcome. Each day and experience will be what you make it. I would like to use this final trip to Italy as an example.

After a stressful week of exams in Ireland, I decided I needed to get away. I wanted a change of scenery for a while and frankly, I did not care what end-of-the-semester school responsibilities I should have been paying more attention to. I let all that go to instead go on one more trip before I left Europe. And let me tell you what, I fell in love.

I think I fell in love with this trip so much because it was full of such joy, laughter, and disaster. In other words, it was not a perfect trip by any means. But I am so glad it was not, because a trip that always follows the script is not an adventure. And I am learning that what I love are true adventures.

My trip started with me leaving Cork at 1:00 a.m. on Tuesday morning. I was initially supposed to be picked up by a taxi at 12:40 a.m., but that would have been too easy. Instead, the taxi apparently forgot me, because it never showed up. I now had 20 minutes to get downtown to catch a bus that was leaving at 1 a.m. Let me repeat, I had 20 minutes for a walk that took at least 30 minutes (hence why I was getting the taxi). But even though I was feeling a little hopeless at that point, I took off sprinting anyway because I really wanted to go to Italy.

So there I was running through the streets of a desolate Cork with my fifteen-pound backpack and my ten-pound rain boots (at least that is what they felt like). I am sure I was a sight to see, but luckily there was no one around to see me. I mean, I did not blame them; it was only 30 degrees outside. But instead of freezing, I personally was sweating and sucking air. I learned in the span of five minutes just how out of shape I was.

I was also dropping everything. I dropped my jacket, my headphones, my pen (twice), and my purse. Honestly, I was surprised I did not fall myself. Though I stayed upright as I ran along, I knew there was no way I was going to make it in time. So, I decided to look around for a solution. Looking back, I cannot believe I even followed through with my first option.

In my moment of desperation, it just so happened I saw an ambulance driving along on the empty streets of Cork. So, what did I do? Of course, I asked if he could give me a ride. Did I mention I was desperate?

He was really kind, but told me that unfortunately he could not because he had a patient on board. I am sure, though, that in my state (sucking air, lungs on fire, heart pounding, asking an ambulance driver for a lift) he might have been thinking that actually I should have been the patient in the back on my way to a different type of facility.

At that point, I had ten minutes before my bus left and not a clue what I was going to do. Luckily as I kept running, I finally found a taxi parked outside of a pub. I mean, you have to love the Irish and their late closing times. I jumped in the taxi, breathlessly told the driver I needed him to hurry to get me to the bus station, and tried to normalize my breathing. He was a good sport and asked me if I had slept through my alarm. When I told him no, that actually the taxi forgot me, he started laughing. When I informed him who my second option for a ride had been, we both busted out laughing. Thankfully, he put the pedal to the metal and got me to the bus station with two minutes to spare; though it took me about 20 minutes to get my breathing back to normal after he dropped me off.

After the four-hour bus ride, I arrived in Dublin at the airport. But along the way I ran into something the Irish say never happens. I ran into snow. First there was a hurricane, and now a snowstorm. What are the odds that in a country where these two things rarely happen, I am there for both? I definitely cannot say this experience abroad was boring.

I flew out around 6:00 a.m. and got to Bergamo by 10:00 a.m. I then caught a bus to Milan and left Milan by train to get to Bologna. I was surprised at how smoothly these transfers were going, so somewhere in the back of my mind I knew I was starting to run out of luck.

I finally made it to Bologna at 1:30 p.m. and the timing could not have been more perfect. I was meeting a friend who lives there and just as I started to exit the train station, she turned the corner and we ran into each other. It was so good to see Elena because I had not seen her since high school when she did an exchange program at my school. As we started walking the streets of Bologna, I was amazed at how beautiful it was. Elena also treated me to the local cuisine for lunch, which was beyond delicious.

We walked around for the rest of the afternoon. I was in heaven as we ventured into libraries, museums, churches, universities, and so much more. There were also Christmas lights and Christmas markets all over and everything just looked so magical. I could not have asked for a better afternoon spent with a dear friend as my tour guide.

That night, we went back to the convent where Elena lived and where I would be staying. Yep, that is right. I stayed at a convent. And it was the coolest experience ever; like I was actually living the Sister Act dream. I mean there were no nuns singing "I Will Follow Him" or "Oh Happy Day," but the nuns were extremely inviting and honestly so funny.

After getting settled in my room, I had the opportunity to eat dinner with Elena's friends, who turned out to be some of the nicest people I met during my time abroad. We joked and laughed about differences in America and Italy, and honestly just took the opportunity to share our knowledge of the world with each other. I loved listening to them go off on tangents in Italian even though I had no clue what they were saying. But they were always so kind to say something and then be like "What I said was . . ." and translate for me in that way.

Over the course of the night, we continued to converse in both English and Italian. One of Elena's friends could not speak English. We kept laughing because even though I shared I could not speak Italian, she thought that if she spoke slower and louder at me, I would be able to understand her. A few times, it had us in tears. As I sat there listening to their conversations, I realized that while I may have started out that day dropping things in Cork, I ended the day picking up new friendships, new sightseeing experiences, and a few Italian words in Bologna.

The next day I took off at 7 a.m. and walked to the train station to catch a ride to Florence. I had to switch trains, which proved a little trickier than I thought, but somehow it all worked out. In other words, I was still crushing the transfers.

When I got to Florence, I started walking around and snapping picture after picture because everywhere I looked it was so beautiful! The architecture was out of this world. I also ate amazing local food that literally melted in my mouth.

Hands down, though, the best moment was when I turned a corner and literally just stopped as my mouth fell open. I had accidentally just run into the huge dome and cathedral Florence is known for; it quite literally took my breath away. I have never seen anything so massive or beautiful as the Santa Maria del Fiore cathedral. I decided to grab some gelato and just revel in the beauty while I stood there and stared at it. It was a true Italian experience.

I then decided to take off on a hike to overlook the city. The view from my vantage point was absolutely incredible and there was even a double rainbow that encapsulated the town. It was the perfect reminder I needed of God's promise to always see us through our storms.

I stayed in Florence until late in the evening so I could look at all the Christmas lights and decorations. I could not take pictures because my phone had died, but I think it made me appreciate the beauty even more. I also got to watch a light show on the famous Ponte Vecchio bridge and eat more gelato. My heart was content.

I finished the day by taking a late train back to Bologna and was proud of myself that I somehow managed to find my way back to the convent in the dark. Elena was so sweet and made a homemade dinner of pasta for me that night. I really felt like I was living the Italian dream.

Sadly, I had to say good-bye to Elena early the next morning. I caught a 6:00 a.m. train to Venice . . . although I almost did not.

Since my departure time was so early, I had to leave the convent in the wee morning hours. There of course was no one to let me out of the convent at that time, so I had to let myself out. Everything was going fine until the wooden gate slammed shut.

Suddenly, there was a man and his very large German Shepherd standing five feet from me. And let me tell you, that dog started going crazy. He was barking and growling and his owner was struggling to hold him back. All I could think was this is it. It all ends here on the streets of Bologna. It has been fun. Sorry mom, I broke our promise that I would return home alive. I also found it fitting that God would call me home right outside of a convent.

But apparently God was not ready for me yet. I somehow managed to get past the man and his dog and took off speed walking. As I was walking the city streets alone in the dark, I was beginning to realize that this was becoming a trend. Sometimes I question my own fearlessness.

The train ride to Venice was without incident. Once I arrived, I took off on foot to explore the city. However, it was not but five minutes before I was hopelessly lost. Venice is hands down the most confusing place I have ever seen, and I was foolish enough to think I could navigate it without a map. I was weaving in and out of very narrow streets and getting myself deeper and deeper into a mess.

As I continued to wander aimlessly, I began to really miss Elena. I could not communicate with many of the locals because they did not speak English. If I did manage to find someone who could speak a little English, it was not much help because they would give me like two directions and then tell me to ask someone else for directions at that point. Basically, they knew how confusing their city was. I also knew I was getting myself more and more lost in the maze of streets when all I could hear was strong Italian accents alternated with silence.

Here is a travel tip for all of you. In a city that claims to be flooded by tourists, if you go thirty minutes without seeing a tour group (usually Japanese, Chinese, or American) and you hear more silence than noise, you probably are going in the very wrong direction. That is the lesson I learned after not seeing a soul for 20 minutes.

But now, getting lost was not all bad. I was able to ask a good looking young Italian man for help with directions and he kindly obliged. He even led me half-way to my destination and was honestly the reason I found my way in the end. I might have to rethink coming home with an Irish husband.

When I finally made it to the main square known as the Piazza San Marco, my breath was again taken away. It was magical. And even though a walk that should have taken me 30 minutes took me almost two hours, I was so in awe I did not care. I grabbed some food and then some gelato. I wanted to make it a tradition of eating gelato while staring at Italian architecture that made my jaw drop.

After about three hours of walking around, I bought a Vaporetto ticket so I could cruise the canals of Venice. Even though Elena had warned me it might be a waste of money, I did not want to get lost again in the city streets, as I surmised missing my bus and flight would be an even bigger waste of money. And honestly, the canal experience was breathtaking. I rode standing up in the back so that I could take pictures and videos of gondolas and boats going down the canals. I simply ignored the fact I was freezing because that was a once in a lifetime opportunity.

Unfortunately, the tail end of the Vaporetto trip was when my luck of making smooth transitions with my transportation ran out.

It started when I accidentally got off on the wrong stop on the Vaporetto. In my defense, it was not entirely my fault. I got off at the bus stop location, which apparently, I should not have. Luckily, I had about 45 minutes to find my way because I needed it.

A police officer kindly told me I needed to take the "People Mover" to the other side of the island. I proceeded to walk in that direction and saw there was a walking path. So, sarcastically in my head, I was like, "I don't need the People Mover, I am the people mover."

Worst mistake.

I spent the next twenty minutes hitchhiking across a major highway that all would have been bypassed if I had taken the People Mover. I was honestly just praying at that point I was heading in the right direction. I will admit I began to question it a little bit when I started walking in a sketchy warehouse district after a while.

About ten minutes later, I finally saw the green bus I was supposed to be on. And I still had 20 minutes to spare. Sometimes I am amazed at how things work out.

From Venice, I had a three-hour bus ride back to Bergamo and then flew out that night at 9:00 p.m. On the plane, I ended up sitting between an older Irish man and a middle-aged Italian man. Soon they were Gene and Marco to me, and we were all sharing laughs and stories about each of our cultures and where we lived and grew up.

As I switched between conversations with the two men as the flight went on, I gained pieces of wisdom from both. Marco told me the best way to learn a foreign language was to have a foreign boyfriend and Gene told me what drinks to have when going to the pub. It was really all the essential information I needed to know. Marco further taught me to always be an optimist and Gene taught me to keep my sense of humor, especially when I am older. It was such a pleasure meeting both of them. Gene also gave me a hard time saying I was either the bravest or one of the most foolish people he knew for trying to navigate Venice on my own without a map. Foolish, Gene, foolish.

As our flight came to an end, our landing ended up being less than smooth because it was so windy in Dublin. After we touched down, I looked at both visibly shaken men and asked if they wanted to join me at the pub so we could all calm down a bit. There really was no shortage of laughter on that flight.

Once off the plane, I had to wait for about an hour in the airport before I caught my bus back to Cork. I finally got back to my apartment at four in the morning on Friday and crashed.

Thinking back, I realized I had a total combined 15 hours of sleep over those four days and walked over 76 miles as I explored Italy. And though I could hardly move that next week because I was so sore, my emotional and spiritual body were thriving.

My trip to Italy truly ended up being a wonderful, final European adventure.

———

It is insane to me that seven years have passed since I lived abroad. Some days it feels like yesterday I was meandering aimlessly around Europe. And then other days, it seems like it was a lifetime ago. But regardless of the time that has passed, the wisdom I gained while living and traveling abroad will forever remain embedded in the fabric of my life.

I sincerely hope as you read through my blogs about Ireland and Europe, you were able to make note of some of the lessons I learned and how you might apply them to your own life. And if you are able to apply the lessons, I pray they end up being as transformative for you as they have been for me over the years.

Before concluding this part, I want to leave you with a quote by Lawrence Block. He states, "Our happiest moments as tourists always seem to come when we stumble upon one thing while in pursuit of something else."

While I would like to believe I turned into more than just a tourist during my time abroad, I believe there is a powerful truth to this quote. I started by sharing how I was in pursuit of a renewed meaning in life when I initially set off for Ireland. During my five-month journey there, I ended up stumbling into joy, laughter, friendship, curiosity, boldness, adventure, and dare I even say love. I do regret to inform you it was not in the form of an Irish husband (though I am still looking). Instead, it was a love for life like I have never felt before.

Therefore, I encourage all of you to continue pursuing what you are truly seeking in life. I promise, you are bound to stumble upon something even greater along the way. Who knows, it may even help you answer that question, "What on Earth am I doing?"

Scan to View Images

PART 3

LIVING OUT MY PURPOSE

"Don't ask yourself what the world needs. Ask yourself what makes you come alive, and then go do that. Because what the world needs is people who have come alive."

—Howard Thurman

Overcoming Struggles and Mastering My Purpose

T he intent of this part of the book is to delve into common questions we all ask ourselves in life and explore how we attempt to overcome challenges when they arise. The secret I will let you in on is that there is no one way to overcome our struggles. I often choose to laugh about mine, as I have demonstrated through my travel blogs. But that is not always easy to do when misadventures happen. And let us be honest, most of us face more challenges in our mundane day-to-day lives than we do when we are jet-setting around the world.

One of the biggest challenges we face is the age-old question of purpose. Discovering it in life is hard. Period.

In fact, I find it ironic we ask children from a young age who and what they want to be when they grow up. The reason I laugh at our tendency to do this as a society is because most adults themselves do not know how to answer this question. (If you do, please come find me and let me in on the secret.) More often than not, if you were to ask an adult, you would likely get a response along the lines of, "I am still working to figure that out."

I think for most of us the challenge with trying to answer this question is that often we do not know what our true purpose is supposed to be. Is it to be the best daughter/son? A good sibling? A trustworthy friend? A hard-working colleague? Or just a decent human being? I believe we often find our identity becomes wrapped up in so many different relational aspects of our lives that it is hard to remain objective about who we truly want to be.

And this certainly is not a question we grapple with in a linear matter. This question seems to revisit and sometimes re-haunt us at various times throughout our lives.

As you will see with the first few blogs that follow, the "purpose" question is one I have personally struggled with at many times in my life. First, I struggled as a college freshman trying to find my way in a foreign environment, and then again as a college senior scared about what the adult world I was about to be thrust into was going to entail. These blogs may seem a bit repetitive when read back-to-back, but my point is to show that whether I was writing in 2016 or 2018, I was struggling with the same quest of finding my purpose. I still am . . . and it is 2024.

As you read the following blogs, take note of any commonalities you have experienced when it comes to identifying one's purpose and pushing through challenges in pursuit of passions. I have no doubt you will relate to at least one aspect of these life quests.

The Bigger Question (*February 2016*)

What do you want to be when you grow up?

That question reverberates all throughout our childhoods and into our early adult lives. As a child, that question is full of wonder and amusement because we get to say something different every time we are asked. But what happens when we get to high school and we have to really start thinking about that question because our choice of college could ultimately determine our career path. Even scarier is when we get to college and are actually having to work towards that goal in order to make it a reality. That childhood dream is now staring us straight in the face and we must decide if that is truly what we want to do.

For me, I have never had a concrete answer to that daunting question. Like my childhood counterpart, I wish I could experiment with multiple professions and fluidly transition through them on a day-to-day basis. But the reality is, life makes us decide what we are going to do. And that can be a challenging task to figure out.

For example, when I first began college, my mind was made up that I was going to major in business. However, after only one short quarter, those plans quickly changed. Now, I am pursuing a degree in Molecular Biology with the hope I can attend medical school to become a surgeon.

But what I have experienced in college so far has not convinced me that attending medical school is the right path for me either.

The reason I have again started doubting my career path is not because the course load is extremely challenging, but rather it is because of the people I am surrounded by. All of my classmates think everything has to be a competition – that they have to be number one. That ultimately, they have to be the smartest person in the room. To them, the only thing running through their minds is, "It's all about how I can stand out!" As a result, they are quick to tear down those around them.

The problem is this is not how I was raised, and it certainly is not what I believe. I hate competition and have never understood why everybody cannot just lift each other up. As a result of these personal convictions, people have begun to tell me the medical school profession is likely not the right path for me because it is cutthroat and competitive.

But does it have to be?

To me, the answer is simple. No.

I say this because I have had a lot of experience in the field of medicine. Not practicing it, but instead actually being the one it was practiced on. Maybe that is why I look at the nature of medical school differently.

While I understand the competitive drive to a degree, I believe too much of it is what makes most physicians believe they are better than everyone else. Of course, when I was a patient, I wanted a great surgeon. I wanted a surgeon that was competent and skillful, who I knew would do a good job. But I did not have to have the BEST surgeon; the one who reached the top only by stepping on others.

The problem I see with these types of individuals, is they lack the humility to connect with others. They forget that their title is just a title. It does not make them better than anybody else, and it certainly does not give them a right to treat people as if they are not equals.

Of course I am generalizing, and this in no way applies to everyone practicing medicine. But the point remains. This superior attitude creates hostile environments in which I am not sure I want to be around.

Unfortunately, though, these types of uncollaborative environments are not unique to just medicine. We see them spanning multiple professions as individuals attempt to race up career ladders.

So, I would implore you the next time you are asked what you want to be, that you not only think about what you want to be, but WHY you want to be it. I hope you find your heart in the right place, and you are not driven by a need to one up others just to be on top in your career.

And as for me, I may become a surgeon, or I may not. But regardless of which career path I choose, I will always hold onto the belief that our innocent childhood dreams were always full of great wonder and humility at what we could one day accomplish alongside each other. Competitiveness be damned.

Searching (*April 2018*)

I feel like ever since I returned from my time abroad, I have been searching for answers in my life. And to be honest, the only place my searching has gotten me, is buried under more questions than I can answer or even comprehend.

One of the biggest questions I have been asking myself lately is what I really want to do when I "grow up." The scary thing about pondering this question and coming up with zero ideas, is that I have about 17 weeks to figure an answer out. Once those 17 weeks come to an end, I am going to be forced to enter the real adult world once I graduate college. Then what? Well, that answer should be easy right? I mean, c'mon Maddy, you went to college to get a degree, so clearly you must have some idea of what job you want to pursue.

But I do not. And it is not for a lack of trying or searching, believe me.

The general conversation that runs through my mind every time I ask myself what I am going to do when I graduate can be quite comical. I often tell myself I can use my Psychology major to go into the Psychology field to help others. Then I laugh.

I laugh at the idea that I have just entertained the thought that I would be effective in a profession where I am expected to help others cope with their emotional and mental concerns.

Really?! As if I do not have enough of my own.

Okay, so maybe that is not the right path. Therefore, I subsequently go to plan B, and the following dialogue is usually what ensues in my head (and sometimes out loud):

"You could use your Molecular Biology major to . . ."

"Yeah, exactly, to do what?"

"Well, you could go into research."

"And spend hour after hour, day after day, sitting in a lab all by myself? Hard pass."

"Ok, well then you could get your Master's degree or PhD in science and become a professor."

"Really? That was the next best thing you came up with? Have you forgotten one of your own cardinal rules? When I say no kids, I mean no kids in the womb and no kids in the classroom."

I generally proceed to come up with many other options, but as you can imagine, there are always reasons I believe those options are just as terrible. As a result, I always find myself right back to asking the same question: What on Earth am I going to do?

Well, maybe I should keep trying to find something I went to school for I think to myself. After all, I have two more options. But if we are being honest, my chemistry minor just came as a package deal with my biology major, and I barely made it through those classes with my sanity intact. I do not think it would be wise for me to pursue a career in that field unless you all want to witness another Chernobyl disaster. In other words, the order in which you add the reagents to a reaction matters. And truth be told, I have never been good at following directions.

Alright, so last option. I have a concentration in cognitive neuroscience. Honestly, this might be the only one worth pursuing further. I love the human brain, but let us not kid ourselves: It is complicated. Shoot, I cannot even make one decision about my future.

Therefore, if I pursue this path, I will probably feel like I chose a career in philosophy where nothing ever makes sense, and where I come up with questions that will never have an answer. I think I have actually already mastered that lately.

So here I am with two majors, one minor, one concentration and zero plans. I think I might have done college wrong.

I have started to believe the reason I keep looking, but missing my destination, is because while I had an interest in all of these areas at one time, that interest is no longer there. And if I am being completely honest, I think what I am really after is trying to find my true calling in life, as I believe it is a shame if we follow anything but our passions.

Then it should be easy, right? Just find what your passion is and follow that.

Well, without blinking an eye, I can tell you what my passion is. My passion is writing.

But even when I identify this passion, why do I act so afraid to pursue it? Why do I come up with as many reasons as to why it is not feasible, just like I do with any of the other career options I have thought about?

It is usually because I tell myself things like, "You will not make enough money doing it," "Your writing is not that great," or "You did not go to college for that, so you have no experience to show." These are just a few of the thoughts that run through my head, but they are enough to silence my passion every time I think about pursuing it.

And I know I am not alone on this turbulent quest of following my passion. But unfortunately, I think what happens all too often is that people settle. The head wins and the heart loses. We go with what we think is the responsible choice or the choice that is going to give us more financial security in the future. As a result, we end up letting our passions die.

We might say we will revisit those passions down the road, or we will keep them kindled on the side. But the truth is, if your passion is not the roaring center of your life, once you turn your back for even a second, that spark can burn out mighty fast. So then, how do we keep that from happening?

When I came across this quote the other day, I kind of got my answer:

"Yes, work towards a degree and work towards earthly friendships, but do so in His name. Chase the author of love and the One who created you first. **How are you supposed to figure out your purpose in this world if you do not first follow the One who created your purpose?** Try your best. Study for the test. Do some squats. But focus fully on His name. And in your weariness, brokenness, and on days when you are overwhelmed, breathe in and breathe out. Then look at where your feet are planted. God put you where you are for a reason. He's gotten you this far. Why don't you trust Him with your tomorrow?"

What this quote revealed to me is God knows our purpose and He is not going to let us go down the wrong path without eventually showing us the right one. Yes, maybe we first go with the "safe choice" and choose the job we do not necessarily like, or want, but feel is our best option at the time. But I guarantee you, if it is the wrong choice,

He will redirect us. There is absolutely nothing we could do that will ruin the plans God has for each of us.

So maybe some of you are still searching for your purpose. Or maybe others of you have identified your passion, but are afraid of the cost of following it like I sometimes am. Whatever aspect you might be struggling with, I would encourage you to remain in pursuit of it no matter the perceived costs, because you never know how stumbling upon your passion might just change your life.

I hope, though, that at the center of whatever purpose you are searching for, you find your God-given worth there. I ultimately believe each of us are destined to achieve what sparks that fire in our hearts.

———

The next few blogs are meant to bring awareness to the fact that we all have struggles in life. None of us are immune to facing challenges when we are in pursuit of our passions and purpose. My hope in sharing mine is that by reading about them, it will inspire you to persevere through yours. Though there were many times I wanted to throw in the towel when I was struggling in college, encountering unfair situations in life, or struggling to keep my head above the water when I was working and going to school full-time to earn my Master's degree, I never did because I knew my purpose was greater than my struggles.

But do not be deceived. The road was hard. The nights were long. The blogs themselves will illustrate just how unpretty it was at times. However, I hope they also serve as a reminder that joy, laughter, and silver linings can still abound, even when everything seems to be falling apart.

———

Laughter is the Only Medicine (*January 2016*)

We have all heard the saying, "Laughter is the best medicine."

From my experience, that line could not be more accurate. My cares and worries seem to melt away as my stomach tightens and my body is racked with laughter. But the problem is, when I reflect back on my life since starting college, I have found myself with more worries and cares than I have ever had before. And that is when it came to me: I do not laugh anymore.

I used to laugh every day. It could have been the result of a funny encounter, a blooper moment in my life, or just a good inside joke with a friend. Now, I am pretty sure those tears of laughter have turned into tears of sadness and frustration as I am struggling to find my way. But I do not want you to think it is all bad. Those tears have led me to discover a great college tip: laminate your notes, and your tears will roll right off.

But in all seriousness, laughter has been hard to come by these past few months, and even when I do manage to laugh, I am usually alone in doing so. It is like a comedy show for one, where I am both the jokester and the one being ridiculed.

But what I have come to discover, is that being both is ok, because ultimately laughter should know no bounds.

Let us take yesterday for instance. I got a text in the morning from my sister, and after reading it, I could not stop laughing. It read something along the lines of, "I fell going up both flights of stairs this morning. So how is your Thursday going?"

Please understand I love my sister dearly and truly care for her safety, but at that time, all I could do was laugh uncontrollably as I continually pictured her falling UP the stairs instead of DOWN them. As this moment was unfolding, I noticed I instantly felt better because the laughter allowed me to release some of the tension I had been holding onto.

Now I am not so naïve to think it is always going to be easy to laugh about any and everything, because sometimes our hardships are simply not funny. But I would encourage you to try to laugh at your mishaps as often as you can because life was never meant to be as serious as we sometimes make it. So, on the days when the last thing you feel like doing is laughing, I would challenge you to find a reason to do so.

In the event you have not laughed today and could use one, I want to share a joke with you before concluding this post. The joke reads, "A blonde and a brunette are in a car and the brunette mentions that Christmas falls on a Friday this year. The blonde responds that she hopes it is not the 13th!"

Though I admit this joke is rather corny, I hope I managed to at least put a smile on your face or maybe even a laugh in your heart.

Just remember, that much like the bug and the windshield, sometimes you are the joker and sometimes you are the joke. What truly matters, though, is that you find the ability to laugh when you discover yourself in either position.

Thus, my final charge to you is to find something to laugh about every day. I promise you those tears of laughter that fall down your face (and occasionally down your leg) will find ways to lighten your mood and your heart.

So while some might claim that laughter is the best medicine, I contend it is the only medicine.

Since it comes from within, it heals from within.

Where Is Waldo and My Identity? (January 2021)

Can I go back to 2020? Did you ever think you would hear someone say that?

Well after this last week, those were my sentiments exactly. But after reflection, I quickly realized my misfortunes could be turned into a funny story with the hope it could make some people laugh if they have experienced similar situations. Or at the very least, I could teach others a lesson before they do experience anything similar.

So, what could have been that bad?

Well, it started when I learned the mailroom at my apartment complex had been broken into. And let me tell you, the perpetrators did a number on it.

The thieves used a crowbar to break open every single block of mailboxes in the locked mail room. They then proceeded to steal all of the mail in them. One of those mailboxes was mine, and let's just say that it had some stuff in it. I know those of you who know me are not surprised by this confession, as you know that sometimes I do not collect my mail for weeks. But nonetheless, I knew I was in trouble when I found out the news. How much trouble, though, would come to light later.

What I knew right away was I had lost a package that had been in my mailbox containing a sweatshirt I had been anxiously awaiting. You might think, big deal, it is just a sweatshirt.

But let me provide a little background about this particular sweatshirt. I placed the order for it back at the very beginning of December from a company I thought was based in the United States. However, I quickly learned the sweatshirt would be coming from China.

For the last two months, I have tracked this package across the world. I am pretty sure I watched it sail up and down the South China Sea and then back up again. It then had a brief stopover in Egypt to see the pyramids before landing in the United States sometime in early January. However, I then watched with amusement as it oddly flew back to China (it must have been looking for its friend it left behind) and then came to Florida. From there, I watched it fly to Texas and then California, where it was finally handed over to a local courier that I later learned was USPS. I am telling you, this package gave me the true, "Where is Waldo?" experience. Once in Colorado, the sweatshirt finally arrived in my mailbox on January 22nd. Ten hours before the theft of all days.

Since I failed to pick up my mail that day, and thus subsequently lost my package, I first wanted to cry. But all I could do was laugh. I mean I could only imagine the number of planes, trains, buses, ships, cars, camels, and who knows what else this package traveled on to make it within 500 feet of my apartment door to only get stolen on the day it arrives. It really was like finding Waldo and then having him get kidnapped from right under my nose.

As there was not much I could do except report the theft, I went ahead and filed a police report. Or let's say, I tried to file a police report.

Given I live in Littleton, I first tried to file a report with the Littleton Police Department. I quickly got a reply back saying my address was not in their jurisdiction, and that I would need to file my report with the Denver Police Department. Slightly confused, I proceeded to do just that. A couple hours later, I received a message back from the Denver Police Department saying they rejected my report because it was not in their jurisdiction and instead, I needed to file with the Littleton Police Department. What?!

Thoroughly confused at this point, I called one department and asked them to set up a conference call with the other department to get my issue sorted out. I mean, clearly I was located in one of their jurisdictions. As I listened to the two departments haggle with one another over this issue, I again could not help but laugh. Sitting there listening, I felt I was privy to a reenactment of Abbott and Costello's "Who's on First?" as confusion was clearly the only topic of conversation. I came to the conclusion that Waldo was just not going to be found and that possibly the police, of all people, were aiding and abetting him.

I wish I could say my troubles ended there, but I cannot. As I continued to think about why anyone would hit our mailboxes at this time, a sickening realization struck me. Tax season was approaching, and we all know what that means. All W2s (you know those things that have your social security number on them) have to be postmarked and in the mail by the 31st. Being that I switched jobs last year, that meant I would have two in the mail from my different employers. The problem was that my mail did not end up in my hands.

Filing a missing person's complaint over Waldo thus quickly became the least of my concerns. Now I had to worry about my identity being stolen. Fear seized me for the better part of the week, but honestly, what could I do about it? The mail was gone, and that fact was not going to change.

So, I looked for the silver lining. I started to hope that if somebody did have my identity, then they would at least make it a fun ride together. I mean, given I had been living like a 90-year-old cooped up in my apartment for the past year because of COVID, I was due for a little excitement. The possibilities in my mind became endless. Maybe "I" would open an account in the Cayman Islands and buy a private resort in the Bahamas. You know, anything adventurous where I could vicariously live through my identity stealers. But alas, no such luck. I am sad (yet relieved) that in the end, no new lines of credit popped up.

Now was any of this particularly funny at the start of the week? Absolutely not. But it taught me valuable lessons.

First, it taught me the practical lesson that I should get my mail every day. To many, this is a no-brainer. But it was not for me because I never imagined that my mail, which is double locked, could ever get stolen. Yet hindsight is always 20/20, especially when crowbars come into play.

More importantly, though, what it taught me is that even when I cannot control what is happening around me, I can challenge myself to control the way I respond to it. That is where my power lies. Therefore, I could choose to be bitter or angry that all this happened, or I could laugh about it and turn it into a story I will never forget.

I have chosen to go with the story. And while I sincerely hope none of you ever find yourselves in a similar situation, I pray that if you do, you can spin it into a fun story as well. Because while it is inevitable that we are going to face hardships in life, I for one, am ultimately thankful that my blessings are bigger than my problems. And that remains true even on weeks where it seems there is one problem after another.

Struggling? Me Too (October 2019)

A cold, snowy Sunday afternoon seemed like the perfect excuse to curl up with a blanket and write. Write for fun I should say, because there has been no shortage of writing in my life recently. Writing for my master's program has turned me into a human typewriter these last seven weeks.

However, when I finally sat down to write today, I struggled with what to write about. Seems fitting, I thought. Struggling appears to be a common theme in my life right now. But then I realized, why not write about that? So that is what I am going to dedicate this post to doing.

In choosing to share my struggles, though, it is important you understand I am not looking for sympathy or pity. I just simply want others to know there is nothing wrong with feeling this way. I think too often we are ashamed to admit we are struggling at times, even though that pretty much describes how most of us are feeling. Therefore, I want to be the one who is not afraid to talk about it.

In order to do that, I have to share my recent struggles, which you may or may not relate to. If you do, that is great. If not, I understand. And again my message is not about doom and gloom, so please feel free to laugh along the way because my struggles have had me rolling at times. After all, I always say, if you cannot laugh at yourself, then you are taking life too seriously.

To give a little background regarding my recent struggles, it mostly has to do with the fact I recently started my master's program. Working full time and going to school full time has been a "struggle" to say the least. I work all day to come home and do school all night, and I repeat this day after day.

Now I was doing fine with this routine (or so I thought) for the first four weeks of school. Then week five hit. And trust me, if there were rewards for struggling, I would have won every single one that week.

It first started with me becoming sick and throwing up a total of six times over the course of Sunday night through early Monday morning. As I laid on my bathroom floor with my pillow and blanket, all I could think was this is how it was going to end and how they were going to find me. I never thought I would go out on a bathroom floor in the fetal position.

On Tuesday, I started to feel better and had a lot of work to make up both for my job and for school. I did my best to get as much done as I could, but I was still flat exhausted. When I got home that night, I put some pasta on the stove and started working on a school assignment. Somewhere in between me starting dinner and starting to type, I fell asleep literally on top of my keyboard. I am pretty convinced I would have slept the night away if it had not been for the smell of burning pasta sauce that woke me up. As I cleaned the slobber off of my keyboard, I decided cereal was going to have to cut it. At least I did not think I could screw that up. Yet with the way my week was going, I would not have been surprised if I had found my milk was sour.

Unfortunately, I did not get to bed until 1:00 a.m. that night/morning, and I forgot to set my alarm. I ended up waking up at 7:15 a.m., which was great because I was supposed to be to work at 7:00 a.m. I did not panic too much because I knew my patients would not be there until 8:00 a.m.

I got ready as fast as I could and got to work. I was pretty proud of myself when I walked in at 7:57 a.m. That was until I realized I drove to the wrong place. You see, I primarily work at one location, but there are days when I have to work downtown. That was one of those days. Realizing I was now going to be very late to work with Denver traffic, I had to call my boss and have "that" conversation. It really just was not shaping up to be my week. I especially felt bad about being late to clinic because I knew I was also going to have to leave clinic early to get to class that night.

When 5:00 p.m. rolled around, I took off to get to school. I was pleased I got to campus with plenty of time to spare before my 6:00 p.m. class. I decided to read in my textbook as I sat in the classroom alone. It was not until about 5:50 p.m. when nobody was showing up that I started to get a little concerned. I checked my phone to make sure it was in fact Wednesday, as that is the night I have on-campus class. I was assured it was and figured everyone was just running late. However, by 5:55 p.m., I started to think something else was up. I checked my syllabus and remembered that two weeks prior, my professor had cancelled class for that night. I had simply just forgotten. As I sat in the classroom alone, I busted out laughing. Somehow in the same day I had managed to be at the wrong place at the right time and then at the right place at the wrong time. That was a whole new level of "struggling."

As I drove home, I was tempted to just keep driving off into the sunset. Because while I do not know about you, I do know some days I have thought about running away more as an adult than I ever did as a kid. That day was one of those moments.

Lying in bed that night, I ended up wondering if all this "struggling" is worth it. I easily could not have gone back to school to get my master's in Healthcare Administration, and maybe my life would be simpler.

But then I would flash back to conversations I have with my patients where I listen to them talk about how much they struggle with our current healthcare system. It breaks my heart listening to their stories. Therefore, I want to do everything in my power to make a difference. I have also had managers tell me they are not in the healthcare business to care about people's feelings, and that is the exact opposite of what I want this field to stand for.

So, while I occasionally struggle with all of my responsibilities on a weekly basis, I know that if I am working towards lessening the burden of others' struggles, that makes mine all the more worth it. And while there might be days I question if I am going to make it through or not, there are never days I question if what I am doing in life matters. I know that even from my limited experience, the work we all choose to do does make a difference.

So just remember, that while struggling is inevitable, giving up is optional. Do not let your struggles hold you back or define you.

Instead, grow resilient through them, so that you can become all that you desire and are called to be.

―――――

As you read through the blogs in this section, I hope you were able to note some commonalities about purpose, struggling, silver linings, and laughter.

And I cannot help but ask: Did reading this part of the book help you discover your purpose in life?

No?

Good, me neither.

But the good news is that what I have discovered is there is no required timeline to figuring it out. I once thought I had to have my purpose identified by the time I got to college, then by the time I graduated college, and if all else failed, by the time I entered the workforce. But that is not the case. I am still working every day to identify my purpose, and I am six years into my post-college career.

Now to be fair, I have to admit I have found a way to put my degrees to use in pursuit of what I believe is my current purpose. But have no fear. I am no cognitive neuroscientist or mad chemist. Instead, I am a healthcare operational leader who is dedicated to pursuing my passion of improving the healthcare field. My current role truly is a blend of my passion and purpose. But that is not always the case for others, and that is ok. Degrees and initials do not have to equate to your purpose.

So again, I want to reiterate that purpose has no timeline. Maybe the beauty is we do not need to ever definitively answer what our purpose is. Maybe it evolves throughout our lives as we discover we have more than one purpose. Maybe we should remain as glib about it as our child-like selves.

But though I might not be able to answer what your purpose is, or provide a pathway to discovering it, I can help enlighten you on what purpose is not. Purpose is not random, it is not easy to ignore, and it is not always easy to pursue. And if I want to stress anything else about what purpose is not, it is this: Your purpose will never be found by trying to diminish someone else's.

My parting piece of advice on this topic is that above all else, do not let the struggles you face keep you from pursuing your purpose. Laugh, cry, scream, or do whatever else you need to do to get through your challenges. Just do not give up. Continue to feed the spark within you and I guarantee you will stumble upon your purpose. Just make sure your heart is in it.

Remember, it is not "**WHAT** do you want to be?" but "**WHY** do you want to be it?" That will eventually help you answer what on Earth it is you are here to do.

PART 4

LIVING AND PRACTICING MY FAITH

"Faith is a living, daring confidence in God's grace, so sure and certain that a man could stake his life on it a thousand times."

—Martin Luther

FAITHFULLY
GUIDING MY WAY

Anyone who knows me knows that my faith is the number one priority in my life. I do all I can to live according to the Word and be the example of love Christ called us to be on Earth.

I demonstrate my commitment to my faith by wearing a bracelet around my wrist that states two simple words: "Only Jesus." This bracelet serves as a reminder for me that regardless of what each day brings, I only need to be concerned about doing what serves Him.

But this sole dedication to faith was not always my precedence in the past. Like many other believers, my faith journey has been wrought with challenges and questions as I have grappled with hardships in my life. During those struggles, what often becomes difficult is not so much continuing to believe in God, as it is having faith God will see me through.

What I think this boils down to is my human nature. Though I profess to have faith in God's plan for my life, I also want to be in on said plan. In other words, I want control. Surrendering is hard as I instead want to proactively work to solve my woes.

I have shared previously in this book that I struggled when I went away to college. And subsequently it was these struggles that sparked my journey into blogging as I viewed writing as a form of therapy. But what I have not previously shared is the challenging first few years I experienced in college are also what grew my faith more than any other time in my life.

There were many days I would sit in my dorm room with nothing on my bed but my Bible. I was constantly searching for scriptures to get me through each day as I continuously struggled with perfectionism and the fear of not living up to my fullest academic potential. I would pray for God to release me from those chains and enable me to trust He was guiding my path forward.

The following blogs will highlight what my prayers and thoughts were during these times as I worked to fully hand the reins of my life over to God. I hope they will serve as inspirations for you to do so as well.

———

Forgive Me (January 2016)

Every day I start my morning with the same routine: Snooze the alarm clock until I know that one more snooze might actually make me late to my 8 a.m. class. Today, though, I hit one less snooze and decided to scroll through Pinterest to switch up the routine a little bit.

As I perused the "Quotes" section, my mind could not help but wander to the laundry list of things I had to do today. I started worrying if I would understand the topics presented in my Organic Chemistry class or if I would have enough time to study for my Calculus II quiz before I had to take it. I realized it is hard to get up when these are the first things I think about in the morning.

As I was reluctantly getting ready to swing my legs over the side of the bed, I came across a quote that stopped me dead in my tracks. The quote read, "Forgive me for picking back up what I've already laid down at your feet."

If ever there was a time I felt God speak to me, it was in that moment.

You see, the night before I had prayed to God to help me get through my lecture today and do well on my quiz. As I talked to Him last night, I laid my problems down at His feet and drifted off to sleep.

But as usual, when I woke up, I picked them right back up and started worrying about the day ahead.

Now I know I am not the only one that trusts God to watch over and guard my problems as I sleep, only to feel it is my responsibility to bear their load when the next day arrives. We all like to have some sense of control over our lives.

But what I have discovered is that I cannot, and should not, seek this absolute control.

I think a large part of why I have been struggling so much recently is because at some point in the last few years, I put God in the backseat and have been trying to drive the course of my life on my own. I have foolishly chosen to charge full steam ahead whilst making comments like, "God I got this, but it would sure be nice if you could tag along and maybe step in if it is not looking so good."

But what I have found from this mindset is that I crash every single time. Instead, God needs to be the driver because quite frankly without him I am lost. I find myself going the wrong way down a one-way street.

Therefore, I would be better off to adopt the mindset of, "God you are in control, and I will tag along with you and go where you tell me to go."

I know that God will never lead me in the wrong direction nor let me falter without being there to pick me up. The other cool thing about walking hand in hand with God, instead of making Him tag behind, is that the load becomes a lot lighter because I no longer have to carry it by myself. I know that in due time, I will find a way in which I can let go of it completely.

But for now, God please forgive me if tomorrow I pick up that which I lay at your feet today. Provide me with a gentle reminder that there is no need for me to carry the weight alone because you are always with me.

———

Friends, hang in there with me for this next blog post. It definitely focuses on a more technical concept . . . making me realize how much of a nerd I was in college. However, it also conveys a vital message I want to share about the importance of letting go of control and instead focusing on faith.

―――――

Living in Permanent White Water (*January 2016*)

In one of my leadership courses in college, I had to read an article titled, "Living in a World of Permanent White Water." The article tackled complex macrosystems that are in place in the world today, and discussed how unfortunately it is often the nature of these macrosystems to upset all attempts to get their subparts to run smoothly.

More often than not, these systems are run by socio-technical structures in which human will and human judgement are exercised on behalf of the system's objectives. As one might suspect, turbulence and instability are woven into the macrosystem because it is profoundly affected by the quality of human will and judgement that is overtaking the system. In other words, people are the problem because everyone is canceling out each other's efforts. What we are left with is permanent white water.

Permanent white water can thus be defined as the complex, turbulent, changing environment in which we are all trying to operate.

I learned that it is characterized by five things. First, permanent white water conditions are full of surprises. Second, complex systems tend to produce novel problems that not only are not anticipated, but also not even imagined. Third, permanent white water conditions feature events that are "messy" and "ill-structured." Fourth, white water events are often extremely costly. And finally, permanent white water conditions raise the problem of recurrence.

With all of these issues swirling around us, it is no wonder we lack direction as a society, and that individually we are struggling to find meaning in this world.

But I still believe there is hope, even if the white water in our world is intensifying. The way I see it, the world is in the mess it is in today because of the very thing trying to control it. That would be us, or more namely, human beings. We create our own permanent white water and are drowning ourselves in the process. We feel ourselves trying to come up for air or simply pray that we can just keep our heads above the water.

What we as a society fail to realize, though, is all of these problems we are creating are actually utterly useless because we are all under the watch of the most equipped lifeguard. If we left our hands out of the system and let God place His hands on it, then collectively we would all benefit. The white water might still be there, but it would not seem as big of a problem.

I shared that permanent white water conditions are full of surprises right? Well yes, while that may be the case, that does not mean God does not equip us to effectively deal with those surprises. Permanent white water is meant to take us out of our comfort zones and require things of us we never imagined. However, God promised us that He would never give us more than we could handle without being there to get us through it. And plus, we tend to grow more as individuals when we are pushed beyond our comfort zones. God wants to see us struggle and grapple with things, so that when He reveals the answer to us in time, we can appreciate the knowledge we gain.

Looking now at the second characteristic of permanent white water, it states that complex systems tend to produce novel problems. This one is not hard to figure out why. If human will and judgment are guiding these systems, then we are leaving God out of the equation all together. Problems are going to continue to multiply and get out of control if we think we can do everything by ourselves.

This leads into the third characteristic that permanent white water conditions are "messy" and "ill-structured." Without God, we will always inevitably find ourselves in a mess. If the foundation of everything we do is not rooted in Him, then how can we expect to build a proper structure in our lives. The foundation will give way when the water comes rushing in every time. If we want a firm foundation, we need to start with asking God to strengthen us from within.

We were told from the fourth characteristic that white water events are often extremely costly. Now some individuals might look at this from a monetary standpoint, but that is not how I view it. To me, white water events are costly in that they suck up our time and energy. I know personally when chaos ensues in my life, I get overwhelmed as the waves start crashing down on me. As I start to lose focus, this subsequently causes me to lose sight of my purpose at times. I feel like there is not enough time to accomplish what I think I need to accomplish. In the end, I cost my body rest and peace.

And if I am being honest, after a while, all of these costs add up. I am left feeling like what is the point in all of this? But then I remember that God did not bring me this far to abandon me now. If I look to Him, He will renew and restore me. And the best part is that it does not cost me a single thing. I have two words for that: AMAZING GRACE!

The final characteristic is that permanent white water conditions raise the problem of recurrence. If we try to do things the way we have always done them, then we can expect to get the same results. Similarly, if we try to solve our own problems, we will always end up with the same problems. That is why God is there. He wants us to bring our problems to Him and lay them down at His feet. We are not fully equipped to handle everything, but He is. Take one problem to Him, and I guarantee you will never see it again in quite the same way.

It has always been interesting to me that when people are drowning, they are told to roll over on their backs in order to float. I surmised this advice was an attempt to keep their mouth and nose out of the water. But now I realize it is to keep their eyes focused on the one who can truly save them from above.

So when permanent white water comes cascading into your life and you feel like you are about to go under, ask yourself why. It might be that your focus is on this world instead of on God. I know I have to remind myself daily that my lifeguard walks on water, so I have nothing to fear.

———

The last post regarding my faith I want to share is a blog I wrote shortly after returning from Ireland. While it is no surprise that my time abroad transformed my life, it also radically transformed my faith. I will let you read how below.

———

I Asked God to Help Me Grow; It Started Raining (January 2018)

My study abroad experience may be over, but the lessons I learned from my time in Ireland and Europe will remain with me forever. Even as I sit in my new apartment in Denver, I cannot help but reflect on my adventures overseas these last five and a half months.

Before I left for the study abroad experience, I was in a rut. I had recently lost a huge part of my life, and I was honestly trying to figure out how I was ever going to be happy again. I found myself not only stunting the growth of my personal life, but also the growth of the relationships I had with those around me.

Therefore, when I knew I was leaving for Ireland, I asked God to help me grow through this experience. At the time, I did not know how He was going to help me do that. But I do know the first day I got to Ireland, it started raining. And quite frankly, it never stopped.

But this was a good rain. The cleansing and growing kind. For over five months, I was on cloud nine. I was living life and loving it, and I was traveling the world as if I had no responsibilities. I was meeting new people, trying new cuisines, and tackling obstacles all along the way.

But then towards the end of my study abroad experience, I fell victim to a hard week.

You see, while I had been growing so much in my personal life, there was still one area of my life I was stubborn to change. And that was my academic life.

Towards the end of the semester, I had to start preparing for my final exams. My solution became to fall back on old habits. That meant I ended up literally locking myself in my dorm room for a week straight. I did not see the sun shine (which it rarely ever did there anyways), get fresh air, or interact with the human world for a week. Every day I only made it as far as going from my bed to my desk. I read a textbook cover to cover (honestly the first time that has ever happened) and I typed over 176 pages of notes. In essence, I spent from the time I woke up to the time I went to bed reading and rereading notes and lectures to the point where I could recite them. I even wrote out practice essays on topics I surmised would be on the exam. I mean to tell you, I went all out.

And then the exam day came, and I panicked. Nothing I had prepared for the essays was even a topic on the exam. And just like that, my "plan" went flying out the window. It honestly was one of the worst experiences of my life (or so I thought in the moment and maybe for a few hours . . . possibly days afterwards).

Since I knew I could not have prepared any more than I did, I did not have regrets about that. My problem was that I was too rigid. I had devised a plan, and I could not see past it. I probably easily could have answered or made a good attempt at one of the other essay questions, but because my mind was freaking out about the fact that my "plan" failed, I could not calm down enough to think straight.

And for me, that was devastating because for some unknown reason, I long ago equated the idea that my grades equal my competence. That is why I have never been able to settle for anything less than an A. So, when I walked out of that exam knowing full well that what I just did was not good, I had a deep pit in my stomach. I could play as many "what-ifs" as I wanted to, but that was not going to change what happened on that test and I knew that. I struggled for days with the fact that this test was not going to reflect my academic standards.

So why do I tell you all this? Why do I share with you what is argu-ably one of my biggest insecurities?

It is because I learned that God was not going to let me come home without changing all of me. I was not going to get to pick and choose the parts of me He was going to alter.

When I had been talking with my mom during that study week, she told me something I will never forget. She of course could sense how stressed I was as she saw me slipping back into my old routine. She told me, "I was reading your blogs again the other day and I just do not want you to lose that sense of adventure and carefree and lighthearted attitude that you have found these last few months."

I am not going to lie, I kind of brushed aside the comment at the time, and responded glibly with, "I won't."

But the problem was that I already had lost the "new" me that week. I had retreated back into my academic self and was the strait-laced Maddy again. And if I am being honest, I hate being strait-laced Maddy. I have tried to beat that person out of my head for the better part of the last ten years. Clearly, I have not been very successful.

I often have to laugh when people look at me in disbelief when I say I hate school. They think I could not perform well if that truly was the case. But they have it wrong. The reason I have always hated school is because I felt like I always had to perform well. I always had to get straight A's. Again, somewhere along the line, I internalized the ill-fated message that my grades equate to my worth.

But what God helped me come to realize during my time abroad, is that it was not my competence that failed me that day. It was just my plan for that one exam that failed.

Though it was a hard pill to swallow, I also came to realize that maybe I needed that failure. Ultimately from that experience, I learned that no matter how hard I study for any test, there is only so much I can learn and retain.

So even though I had another exam coming up about ten days after the first, I decided this next test was not going to get the best of me.

And it did not.

Instead, I decided to put all studying on the back burner and take off on a trip to Italy. And while I told myself I would listen to my lectures on the plane or train, I ultimately did not. Instead, I decided to live life, and I ended up learning more on that trip than anything I have ever learned in a room surrounded by four walls.

How did that next test go you might ask? Honestly, it was not that great either. But there was something different about me and how I responded that truly made me feel freedom for the first time in a long time. I just brushed it off and let it go.

There is this song called "So Will I" that spoke to my heart after my tests and time in Ireland. One line of the song talks about how if Jesus was able to choose to surrender, so should we. I learned quickly that if I was going to truly be a different person, I was going to have to surrender my entire being. Not just the parts I wanted, but literally every single piece of me. God was trying to tell me that if I would just surrender fully to Him, there was something better in store. I just needed to forgo my plan for His.

Then another line in the song talks about how if Jesus was able to leave the grave behind Him, then we should be willing to do the same. We cannot know Jesus's mindset while He was in the grave. Maybe He found comfort there. Maybe He had been tired of all the persecution and while in the grave thought, "Finally, it's over." But did He remain there? No. He left the grave behind Him because He trusted that the plan God had for Him was far greater than what could be accomplished if He stayed in the grave. And I think we can all agree that Jesus rising from the dead was the best thing that could have ever happened.

That is where I found myself as well. There was comfort in being the old me. Oddly, there was comfort in believing my grades had to be perfect all the time or I had to be a great academic. However, it was killing me. In Ireland, I found myself in the grave during my exams. So, I had a choice to make. I could remain there forever, or I could decide that I wanted to follow God's plan from there on out and leave the grave and the old me behind. So, I decided to strictly follow His plan, and I can already feel Him rising and lifting me up as I am beginning to discover this new way of life.

Now I am not foolish enough to think it is always going to be easy or I might not slip and retreat into my old ways from time to time. But I assure you, I am giving it my best effort. And I ask that as my friends, you hold me accountable to stay on this path. If any of you see me retreating back to my old ways, call me out on it. I actually prefer that now.

I laugh when people ask me what classes I am taking now that I am back at DU. When I answer with classes like Research Methods, Neuromuscular Pathophysiology, and Introductory Neurobiology (classes I can hardly pronounce, much less understand), I see how it can sound like I am the strict academic again. But my mindset is different.

Instead of worrying about performing well in the classes, I am excited to learn for the sole purpose of learning. And I know over these next few months, I am going to learn so much about life in general with this new mindset I have. Both in and outside of the classroom.

For instance, I just got a new apartment, and I have already learned that I might not be cut out to be adulting in the United States either. I have already blown the breaker, broken my dryer, and misplaced more things than I can count. So stay tuned because I am sure there will be many more unfortunate (but comical) adulting experiences to come.

But that is ok because though I may be failing at times, I am always learning.

As I reflect back on my time in Ireland one last time, I thank God that He made it rain almost the entire time I was over there. In many ways, His rain allowed me to grow like a tree. He watered my trunk, which allowed me to establish a firmer foundation. He watered my branches, which allowed me to further branch out and meet new people. He watered my leaves so that I could soak up more life and His light. And yes, He even watered those stubborn roots of mine, which allowed me to grow in new directions.

And I know I am not finished yet. Maybe this quarter will be the quarter I get a B. And yes, tears may fall. But contrary to what you think, they just might be tears of happiness instead of tears of sadness. Maybe those tears will be shed in joy as I experience true release and freedom from my old ways. And maybe those tears will provide that last amount of water that helps me grow the most.

———

Hopefully, what these blogs illustrate for you is my recognition that I am an imperfect person striving every day to serve a perfect God and His plan for my life. I will be honest, some days that is easy, and some days not so much. But certain days are difficult only because I find ways to make following His plan challenging. In other words, it is on those days that I still find myself seeking too much control, being too hard on myself, or yes, you guessed it, picking up what instead I should have left lying at His feet.

As I noticed this continued tendency to load myself down with far more than what I should be, I decided in 2023 to physically challenge myself to devise a way to release these unnecessary burdens. And as basic as it sounds, it all starts with a carved wooden cross, pebbles, and weights. I will let you in on what I do, in the hope that those of you who are also apt to carry too much on your own, can adopt a similar tactic.

It goes like this. Every time there is a burden on my heart I am trying to carry, I write it down on a little glass pebble. It might read for example, "Job Performance" or "Health Diagnosis." It can be whatever I am struggling with at the time, whether it refers to me or someone I love. After writing on the pebble and praying for God to help me lay this burden down at His feet, I set the pebble at the foot of a cross that stands about one foot tall on a shelf in my house.

The goal is that as I pass by this cross daily, I pray about these concerns and trust God to do His will. But I do not pick them up and carry them.

However, on those days when I do find myself trying to carry out actions to control whatever concern I had written on a pebble, I have

to remove that pebble from the foot of the cross and subsequently place a one-pound weight in my backpack or bag that I often carry around. The idea is this now becomes an unnecessary weight I am carrying, on top of everything else. The more pebbles I do not leave in their rightful place, the heavier my load becomes.

Now following this practice does not mean you cannot worry about the concern you write on a pebble; that would be kind of impossible. It is just when you find yourself worrying and going out of your way to do things to try to control that concern more than you pray over it, that is when you must add the weight to your bag.

For example, if I write "Job Performance" on the pebble, then find my thoughts consumed with, "I worry what X thought of the work I sent them," or "I wonder if I am producing enough results to be considered a valuable member of the team" . . . friends that is when you add that weight to your backpack. And if those thoughts, along with thousands of other similar ones, are continuously going through your mind, maybe add two. I joke, but we overthinkers have all been there. In truth, we probably all are thinking that on our bad weeks, we hope no one tries to pick our backpacks up.

But my point is you will soon find you do not like carrying all of the extra weight. It loads you down. It hurts your back. It makes climbing stairs more challenging. And most importantly, it causes you to focus on the wrong thing.

The goal instead should be to remove those weights from your bag. And you get to do so when you again decide to place the pebble at the foot of the cross. That prayer might sound like, "God, forgive me for being concerned with how others perceive my job performance. Help me to believe I did my best today and trust that you will let my hard work reveal itself." That is a pebble left undisturbed; a weight removed. In essence, the underlying concern might still be there, but I am trusting God to manage it. Because after all, my performance does not equate to my worth.

Many may wonder why I use a glass pebble. Why not just write my burdens on a piece of paper? It is because the pebbles serve as a reminder of how fragile my burdens are in my own hands. When I have to remove that pebble from the foot of the cross, I risk dropping it. And if I drop it, it could break. If it breaks, then I create a mess that I can cut myself on and thus get hurt by. But at the foot of the cross, the pebble is safe. There is no risk of shattering it. It remains intact and unharmful to myself and those around me.

Friends, I implore you to leave your pebbles at the foot of the cross. You do not need to carry your burdens. And as you gradually learn to lighten your load, your back will thank you, and you might even find you have a spring in your step you did not before.

As I conclude this section, I want to recall your attention to the fact I started this part of the book explaining how my faith is the number one priority in my life. I situate it as the forefront in order to remind myself to strive to do all things not for love, but from His love. So if there is anything I pray you take away from this book, it is the following: Endeavor to lay your burdens down at His feet; grow through the rain God uses to cleanse your life; embrace the permanent white water by focusing on the strength of your equipped lifeguard; and trust that on your best day, or on your worst day, God has you all the same because His love and grace never fail.

If you can learn to embrace these truths, I promise your bags will remain light as God guides you in discovering what on Earth He has placed you here to do.

Scan to View Images

PART 5

LIVING WITH
MISSING PIECES

"What we once enjoyed and deeply loved we can never lose, for all that we love deeply becomes a part of us."

—Helen Keller

FINDING MEANING IN HEARTBREAK

The final part of this book is dedicated to delving into the all too familiar feelings of loss and heartbreak that each of us experiences at one point or another in our lives. But I hope to explore and unpack these topics in a more uplifting manner, rather than focus on the negative emotions they generally tend to evoke in us.

Unfortunately, none of us are immune to loss and heartbreak. It can be in the form of lost loved ones, broken relationships, unmet expectations, you name it. The point is, we all experience these feelings in some way.

I cannot really trace back to the first time I experienced heartbreak in my life. But I can trace back to the first time I experienced profound loss. I was in middle school, and it came in the form of losing my mom's dad, who I affectionately called my papa. It was not until I lost him in 2011 from a post-surgical complication that I learned the true feeling of loss. And experiencing that at the time sucked.

But as fate would have it, loss would revisit me multiple times over the coming years. First with the loss of my aunt in 2016, next with the loss of my grandpa in 2019, and then with the loss of one of my closest friends in 2023. Each experience has been profoundly painful in its own right, as most, aside from my grandpa, were completely unexpected. Unexpected loss is particularly challenging to navigate because it has forced me to grieve not only for the lives they lived, but also for the lives they never had the opportunity to live.

Yet despite how easy it may be to focus on all that loss takes from us, I have challenged myself in the last few years to instead focus on what I have gained from the lives my loved ones lived before being called home. Take for instance both of my grandpas. While they gave me many wonderful memories, one physical thing they both gave me are my crystal blue eyes. I am the only one in my family with them. And while my sister might love to attribute it to the milkman, I know the truth of where they actually came from. Every time I look in a mirror, I see them staring back at me.

Therefore, the following blog posts focus on what their losses have added to my life, instead of what has been taken away by their passing. It is not always easy to think from this perspective, but it is much more reassuring knowing our loved ones never truly leave us.

Contained within this section is also a blog I wrote about heartbreak during the 2020 COVID pandemic. I do not think it is a stretch to say that 2020 was a year of loss and heartbreak for all of us. We had to adjust to new restrictions, come to terms with the loss of personal connection, and experience unprecedented concern over the well-being of our fellow human beings. It was enough to break anyone's heart.

But what I hope you will pick up on as you read the following blog posts, is that beauty can come from pain. Healing can be restored from brokenness. Loss can lead to life. And most importantly, our loved ones can and should continue to live on through us.

————

Resting in Your Embrace (*April 2016*)

April 16th.

Since you have been gone, this day has always brought me pain. But something is different this year. The usual gloom is not hanging over me, and in fact, I feel at peace. I feel your peace.

When God called you home five years ago, I struggled understanding why it was your time to leave us. There were words left un-said and memories that just did not feel the same anymore. I missed your infectious smile and the humor that flowed endlessly from your mouth. As I realized I would not get to grow up and share all my experiences with you in person, my heart ached to talk to you just one last time. I wanted to say just one last, "I love you."

But as time has passed and life has moved on, I have begun to come to terms with why God called you home. I know in the last few years of my life that I have needed a guardian angel, and you have never failed to provide the blessed assurance of your constant presence. I remember one dream vividly, right before all of my surgeries, where I was talking with you, and you just sat beside me and wrapped your arm around me. I had never felt anything like that before, and I thought, "This has got to be what perfect peace feels like." And although my anxiety was low going into my surgeries, I just kept thinking that even if something went wrong and I left this Earth, I had the best guardian angel waiting for me. You would take care of me no matter what. And you have.

As I sit here and reflect on the grand time you must be having in heaven, I cannot help but smile with my crooked smile that you loved so much. I know you are in a much better place, and while I failed to understand why God would take you after giving you what seemed like a new start, I have slowly realized he needed you for reasons far greater than I will ever understand. And I have come to accept that maybe He fixed you on this Earth right before your death, so you were ready to fight His battle the moment you arrived. He did not want to lose any time. And I have no doubt you have not let Him down.

I cannot wait until the day I am reunited with you in our Father's Kingdom and can give you the biggest bear hug like you used to always give me. Growing up, you were my papa, my favorite Santa Claus, my biggest supporter, and the one person who never failed to put a smile on my face. Now you are the best guardian angel I could ask for. Speaking of angels, I hope God set the record straight for you that my freckles are angels' kisses and not cow splatters as you always claimed. Even if you still do not believe Him, I will proudly wear the cow splatters because every time I look at them, I think of you.

As I reflect on the impact you had on my life for those 13 years, I cannot help but tear up. But this year, the tears are tears of joy, encapsulated with memories that make my crystal blue eyes shine brighter. The eyes that I got from you. And I cannot help but see your piercing blue eyes staring right back.

Until I see you again, I will rest in your embrace.

Broken Hallelujah (December 2016)

It has been almost a month since I lost you and yet the pain cuts like a knife deeper and deeper every day. I know my mind has not fully grasped the idea that you are gone, and I have come to realize maybe it never will. The profound connection we shared is now missing in my life, and there is a piece of my heart I will never get back. Unlike others, I do not believe time heals wounds, I believe we just learn how to live with the wounded and broken pieces.

As I sit here and watch the snow fall outside the window today, I cannot help but think of you. This was your favorite time of the year, and I know you were eagerly awaiting the first snowfall. I can only imagine, though, that the snow angels in heaven are a sight like no other, so I know God has not disappointed you this year. You are home for Christmas, and that is the greatest gift you can receive, even though those of us left behind struggle to understand your absence at our earthly Christmas this year.

The cold winter months to come will no doubt be accompanied with darkness and despair. But to wish you were back with me would only be selfish. When your wings were ready, my heart was not, but then again, I know it never would have been. I had the pleasure of having you in my life for 19 years, but I was planning on 40 more.

I guess the part that hurts the most is knowing I will miss out on the future we had planned together. What many may not realize was that you were far more than just my beautiful and loving aunt.

You were my up-for-anything adventure friend, my shotgun rider on serene drives through the mountains, and the most accepting and understanding person I have ever had in my life. You were my favorite person to tell jokes to because you would get this light in your eyes, and I could listen to the sound of your belly laughter for days. You reminded me that three months was way too long to go without a deep clean, and you were my personal fashion designer for every important event in my life. So no, I did not just lose an aunt. I lost one of my greatest friends and my rock that I planned on growing up with. There were 40 years age difference between the two of us, but right now there are 40 years of grief in my heart. 19 years was just not long enough, for it was endless love that I planned on.

Leonard Cohen had a point in how he described love. It often is a cold and broken hallelujah. Hallelujah that you are no longer suffering on Earth and are now at peace in His presence. Hallelujah that your chains are gone and you have been set free. Hallelujah that my angel in life is now the angel watching over me. Hallelujah that you are now reunited with your father who you missed so dearly. Hallelujah that you are soaring higher than you ever have soared before. But on this cold December morning, these hallelujahs are professed from a heart that is broken, for a piece is now missing.

But I know where there is deep grief, there is even deeper love. I recognize you never left me, because as long as my heart is in my chest, you will always reside in me. Our future together may look different now, but I assure you that you will live on in me. In this life I will honor you and everything you stood for because I know no greater honor.

Onward and upward Auntie until I see you again. All my love.

If You See Him (*March 2019*)

I know I am two days late for my February post, but then again February only has 28 days, so maybe I can still claim I am right on time. The real reason I am late writing my blog this month is because I lost my grandpa a few days ago. I had the privilege of being able to spend his final days on Earth with him, and there was no place else I would have rather been. While those days were difficult for my family and me, we found comfort in each other and in knowing that grandpa was getting ready to reside in his mansion in Heaven.

On Thursday when I left him, I knew it was going to be the last time I saw him. I did not want to leave, but unfortunately, we do not always get to dictate the events of our lives. As my sister and I drove back to Denver, we relived all of our favorite memories we shared with him growing up. Man, the things he let us get away with. I guess those secrets are safe now as long as Chandler and I can manage to keep our mouths shut.

Sadly, it was not but two hours after Chandler dropped me back off at my apartment that I got a call from my dad letting me know he had passed. I was standing in the middle of Sam's Club when he called, and I remember thinking, "How crazy am I going to look if I spontaneously break out in tears in the middle of the cereal aisle?"

Pretty crazy probably. But I would not have cared because I had just lost one of my heroes. But as I stood there, instead of a wave of despair, a wave of relief and joy washed over me. Relief that he was no longer suffering on this Earth. Joy that he had just grown his wings and was soaring in heaven with loved ones who had preceded him in death.

While I stood frozen in the aisle, I was trying to understand why this mix of emotions was flowing through me. That is when I saw it. My mind had been so focused on what my dad had just told me that I could not register anything else. It was not until I refocused and came back to Earth that I realized I was staring at boxes of Cream of Wheat sitting on the shelf in front of me. I felt the biggest smile creep across my face as I stood there unable to move. One of my grandpa's favorite breakfast cereals had been a bowl of Cream of Wheat filled with raisins. So though he was gone, it was like he was still right there in front of me. In that moment, I knew beyond a doubt he was feeling so content in heaven and it was much sweeter than any raisin he had ever tasted.

As I look back on that suspended moment in Sam's, I realize he was letting me know that if I look, I will see him every day. I will see him in times of sorrow, I will see him in times of immense joy, and I will see him when I cannot see anyone else.

And you will see him too. When you look at a beautiful garden filled with flowers of all colors, you will see him and the countless hours he spent making sure his gardens were well planted and tended to. When you come across a woodworker whittling away, you will see him and the works of art he could turn any piece of wood into. Some of you might even be lucky enough to own the canes, signs, reindeer, Christmas trees, and snowmen he poured his heart and soul into making. When you listen to someone ask what is for lunch and thirty minutes later ask what is for dinner, you will see him and his endless love for food. When you hear someone tell a joke, you will see him and the twinkle he got in his baby blue eyes right before he told the punchline. When you see a grandfather who moves mountains for his family, you will see him and the love he poured into our family.

So when you see that garden, stop and smell the flowers and tell him hi. When you see the woodworker lost in their craft, stop and admire their work and tell him hi. When you pull out those Christmas decorations next year, light them up and tell him hi. When you hear the always hungry man, chuckle to yourself and tell him hi. When you see that twinkle in the blue eyes he gave me, listen earnestly to the joke and tell him hi. When you see a man who loves his family above all else, cherish him and tell him hi.

I guarantee you will see him, so please do me a favor and tell him hi. Tell him hi and that I love him. Tell him that he is in my heart, and I carry him with me in everything I do. Let him know that as much as I miss him, I would not want him any other place than where he is at.

Because I know that as much as I love him, God loves him more.

Breaking My Heart, But Fixing My Vision (*September 2020*)

I believe you would be hard pressed to find someone who has had the 2020 they expected. I know many have felt their worlds have been turned upside down by the events of this year and the carousel never seems to stop turning. While I have felt similar emotions, if you asked me to characterize my experience of this year, it would be the year in which a lot of things broke my heart but fixed my vision.

While most people experienced a slowdown period in March-May, that was not the case for me. Given my job in the medical field, I had to keep reporting to work when most were asked to stay home. As the virus spread, our clinic switched to delivering telehealth services to keep our patients as safe as possible. Given the relative swiftness in which we had to roll this service out, it goes without saying that the process was messy, complex, and often confusing for staff and patients alike. If one could have looked behind the scenes of our clinic, they would have witnessed us running in directionless circles while trying to maintain a six-foot distance. The work became grueling and emotionally draining as we attempted to care for those most at risk for health complications if they contracted the virus.

During this time, I was also enrolled in my master's program full time. Every night when I came home from work, I faced mountains of homework that often kept me up into the early morning hours. Then I would turn around and do it all over again the next day. As I noticed this monotonous routine was causing me to become emotionally overwhelmed, I decided I needed a stress reliever and turned to running. I would come home each night and run upwards of six miles in an attempt to release the pressure-cooker of emotions coursing through my body.

This routine was working well for me, or so I thought, until one night when I was running and suddenly had a shooting pain in my knee like I had never felt before. Barely able to put any pressure on it, I limped all the way home. A trip to the doctor the next day confirmed

I was suffering from IT band syndrome, and I would have to avoid any strenuous activity for the next two weeks. With those words, I felt the first piece of my heart break as all I could think was, "What am I going to do to relieve all this stress?"

My solution was to turn to nightly walking. And boy did it fix my vision. Every night, I would go walking around the time the sun set to marvel in its beauty. After a couple nights of this walking routine, I started to fondly refer to it as my nightly walk with God as I learned the importance of not only talking, but also listening. Through these nightly walks, He helped me realize how I had been running my body ragged with my tendencies to charge full steam ahead at all hours of the day. I came to understand my body needed a break as well as my mind.

This afforded me the opportunity to pause and reflect on many aspects of my life, as I think many others have had the opportunity to do this year as well. One of the things that became readily apparent to me was it seemed I was running away from something. As I began to pick apart my life on those walks, I realized I was running away from being unfulfilled and unhappy with where I was at in that particular moment of my life. Identifying the source seemed like the next logical step, and when God revealed it to me, I almost had to laugh.

One day on one of my walks all I heard was simply, "The problem is your job." Hahaha um excuse me . . . WHAT?!?! You want me to switch jobs in the middle of a pandemic, when job security is at an all-time low? You have got to be kidding.

But friends, let me tell you, when God tells you to move, you move. My resignation letter has since been turned in, I start my new job in less than two weeks, and once again there is a fire of excitement within me that has replaced the draining well I was feeling. I now realize that if I had not injured myself, I would not have slowed down long enough to hear those needed words. And as I have continued these nightly walks, I continue to see some of the most beautiful sunsets that I would have missed if I had kept up my old, hurried routine.

I have also experienced heartbreak this year in the form of lost friendships. I have watched relationships I have built over the last few years come to disastrous ends in the blink of an eye for reasons that are beyond my control or doing. Yet while the pain of the betrayal may sting, the tears that have fallen have cleansed my vision to reveal to me the type of people I want to surround myself with moving forward. I no longer have a tolerance for disrespect or hatred. I want to commit myself to those who empower one another and lift each other up through the good and bad times. The ones who stand with you in solidarity and support. The last thing I have any interest in is entertaining those who tear others down in an attempt to appear powerful or superior. While this may have been a tough lesson to learn this year, I am eternally grateful for this new clarity in my vision. My prayer is that you are all able to surround yourself with the same type of people in your lives as well.

And finally, our country has broken my heart this year. We have been far from the best version of America I desire to be, and every day when I look at our country, I grieve a little more and more. In our country we cannot seem to understand that all human beings should be treated with dignity and respect and that no one is better than anyone else regardless of race, ethnicity, social status, or sexuality. We have further failed to acknowledge that the pursuit of health should be a human right as our handling of the virus has been one misstep after another. We have failed our health care workforce, our teachers, our students, and our essential workers in more ways than one. We let politicians have a larger voice at the table when it should have been public health officials, and we are paying the price for that.

While all of these issues are shattering my heart into pieces, I do not believe it is any small coincidence that I am getting my master's degree in Global Health Management during this pandemic. Being enrolled in this program at this time has fixed my vision for what is possible, not what is current. As I study health systems around the world, I am inspired by their successes and leadership in developing health systems that are diverse and inclusive. I do not necessarily put blinders on in regard to the United States, but my vision is certainly not fixated on our country as a leading example of how to care for others. So in a way, I appreciate our country breaking my heart, because it has only motivated me more to focus my vision and resolve on building a world through my work that will lift up and not oppress our future generations.

While I have shared my perspective, I am sure many of you have other issues that have broken your heart yet fixed your vision this year. I invite you to share those with me or with others. I think it is important that we celebrate each other's triumphs and lend an ear to others' troubles because 2020 has certainly been a year of both. But I think that is the beauty of this year. For every piece that has broken my heart, something else has come along to mend it.

So while my vision is far from 20/20, I know it is slowly coming into better focus as my heart breaks and mends itself along the way. I hope the same can be true for all of you.

Stay safe and practice love.

Rebirth From Devastation (*March 2023*)

As I sat down to write this blog post today, I found myself reflecting on the concept of rebirth. Seems fitting, I thought, as Spring is in the air. But for me, it is a little bit more than that this year.

While it is not out of the ordinary for me to express vulnerability in my blog posts, this one tugs on my heartstrings a little bit more. But this post is not meant to be sad, instead I am aiming for it to be a more hopeful one. I will let you decide if I succeed in this endeavor.

The idea for this blog started last weekend when my parents came to visit me in Missouri. It was so great to see them after so long and to have the opportunity to spend quality time together. One activity we decided to do along with some friends from St. Louis was go to the Winston Churchill Museum in Fulton, MO. This museum was absolutely incredible! We spent three hours there and easily could have spent another three. Who knew there was so much to offer in my backyard.

While I think Winston Churchill was a beyond inspiring individual, what captivated my attention the most during the tour was the church that is situated on top of the museum. The church is the Church of St. Mary the Virgin, Aldermanbury. The church was originally built in London and then burned down in the Great Fire of London in 1666. It was then rebuilt by Sir Christopher Wren in the 17th century before again being destroyed by the Blitz during World War II. Three centuries later, every piece of the church was shipped to Missouri to be rebuilt in Fulton.

At this point you are all probably thinking, "Geez Maddy, thanks for the history lesson we did not ask for. Where are you going with this?"

That is a great question, so I will get to the point.

While I could tell most individuals during the tour were captivated by the history that was all around us, I was entranced by what the church symbolically represents. Namely, rebirth from devastation. As I stood in the church, I began to experience a kindredness with the centuries old structure; a feeling I have never experienced before.

I related to the church so much in that moment because I am currently learning how to rebuild my life from devastation. At the start of this year, I lost a childhood best friend to suicide. The guilt and blame that has racked me since that day over the events of the situation has been suffocating at times. Not unlike what I am sure the church felt as it was set ablaze.

But as I stood in the church last Saturday, my hope of life from devastation was renewed. The church is a beautiful representation of the human spirit and our unique ability to overcome tragedy. We, like the church, can rise from the ashes and stand tall again in a show of resilience and strength.

So while some days I may feel the battle has been lost, I have to remind myself the war is not over. Nor does it have the final say. We do. Eventually, wars end, but the church is the perfect example that beautiful things live on. That is why I know my friend will too.

I share this experience with all of you because I know we all carry heavy burdens in this life. As you reflect on what rebirth might look like in your own life, I implore you to draw inspiration from this church. And if you ever want to tour it yourself, I have plenty of guest room for you to stay.

I want to leave you with one last thought. As Spring is now upon us and everything starts to come back to life, I hope the flowers remind you why rain is so necessary. I pray your rainy seasons will help you eventually bloom too.

Sending love and light to all of you.

They Will Remember (April 2024)

A few weekends back, I found myself needing to make a trip to St. Louis. But before arriving at my final destination, I decided to first stop and spend some time in Forest Park. For those who have never been, Forest Park is hands down one of the most beautiful urban parks in the country. To put it in perspective, picture a serene landscape complete with forests, nature reserves, diverse ecosystems, and a number of cultural institutions. Truly the ultimate place to both engage and relax your mind.

For me personally that day, I was seeking the latter. After a number of stressful weeks and knowing that big decisions loomed ahead of me, I could sense I needed a mental recess and figured Forest Park was as good of a place as any to offer that.

When I arrived, I was pleasantly surprised to find the park was relatively quiet. That meant I would have my fair share of choices when it came to park benches to sit on. As I started walking along the pavement, I spotted a bench half in the shade and half in the sunlight. Having found my desired spot, I settled in, closed my eyes, and began letting my mind and body relax.

It was not but two minutes into this calming routine when I felt a gentle tap on my shoulder. As I opened my eyes, I was greeted by a warm smile and a wave from a gentleman I estimate was somewhere in his eighties. He introduced himself as Buster (though with the twinkle in his eye, we both knew he was joking) and asked if he could sit a while. I of course obliged, despite the vast number of open park benches around us.

As he sat down, I told him my name was Patricia (with the same twinkle in my eye) and we fell right into conversation. He shared with me that he used to always visit Forest Park with his late wife as they would spend every Sunday meandering along the trails. She had passed the year before, but he tried as often as he could to still come to the park to honor their tradition. His love was evident in the way he talked about her, and I could have sat and listened to him tell stories of the life they had built together all day long.

About 20 minutes into our conversation, he asked me if I was a regular at the park, and if not, what had brought me there that day. As I sat there contemplating his question, I realized I had not been there for about five months, having last spent a relaxing afternoon there with one of my closest friends back in November. "No, Buster, I am not a regular, but as to the second part of your question, I guess I sensed a need to visit the park today," was the response I heard myself giving.

Of course, he was not going to let me off the hook that easily. I ultimately ended up sharing how life had felt rather chaotic for the last few months and the park felt like a good place to quiet my mind. I explained about the continual remorse over the loss of my friend last year, how I was sitting there fresh on the heels of just moving into a new home and settling into a new job, and how I have been working every day to juggle a number of priorities with decks that often seem stacked against me.

Now afraid I had shared too much, I cautiously threw a glance in his direction, only to be met with the widest grin. "How long have you been keeping that in?" he asked, after which we both proceeded to laugh for a solid 20 seconds.

We ended up sitting there talking about life, loss, and everything in between for the next two hours. There was not necessarily anything profound about our conversation, but rather it was raw and honest, and I could tell it was what we both needed at that moment. Both of us were still working to come to terms with loss and what you do with all the love and grief that remains when a person is gone. Those thoughts also brought to mind our own mortality, and on the bench that day, both an eighty-year-old and a twenty-six-year-old brainstormed what a life well spent looks like.

(We also brainstormed better fake names to come up with in the future.)

Though I did not want to leave this kind and humorous man, the time eventually came that I needed to be on my way.

As I stood up to leave, I will never forget the words Buster told me.

"They will remember Maddy."

A bit perplexed, I gave him a quizzical grin.

He explained, "Your friends and family will remember the way you always listened. They will remember that you always cared. They will remember that you always showed up and put them before yourself. You listened to an old man talk about his life and late wife for the past two hours as if his stories were the only thing in life that mattered to you today. If you give that kind of love and attention to a stranger, I cannot imagine the depths you give to your family and friends. So do not worry, when you are no longer around, they will remember. And that is the greatest gift you could ever give them."

As I pushed the lump rising in my throat back down, I hoarsely asked him, "How did you know?"

Now it was his turn to return the quizzical grin.

So I explained, "How did you know that was what I was struggling the most with when I first sat down on this bench today? How did you know that I question if I am prioritizing the right things in my life and if I am showing up in my relationships the best way I know how?"

He did not have an answer, but instead he had another question.

"Why did you pick this particular bench to sit at today?"

After a moment's thought, I responded, "I guess it sort of stood out to me. I was struck by the fact that it was half in the sun and half in the shade. It reminded me that life is made up of both light and dark moments and our job is to simply look for the beauty around us no matter our circumstances. That no matter if I feel the sun on my face or the cool breeze on my back, I should choose to only focus on the joy the beauty surrounding me provides."

"Why did you choose this bench?" I asked in return.

"Because it was our bench for the last 12 years."

Friends, sitting on that bench was not a coincidence. That conversation was not a coincidence. It was a reminder that while we all worry we do not have enough time for everything in life, the truth is, we do. We have the exact amount of time we are supposed to. So do not waste it wishing for more. Instead, fill the time you have with the things and people that speak to you. Take time for walks in the park. Take time to sit and talk with strangers for hours. Take time to tell the people you love that you love them.

And while it is true in life that you will find yourself shrouded in both light and darkness, remember that the sun will rise, and the sun will set. Light and dark are ever-changing.

Time, though, is the one thing we do not get back. So, choose today how you want to spend the remainder of yours. I would encourage you to spend it being the light in someone else's darkness.

———

I surmise that as many of you read the blogs in this section, you found yourselves reflecting on the significant losses in your own lives. Some of those losses you may have come to terms with, and some you may still be struggling to understand. That is perfectly okay because there often is a range of emotions tied up in each loss we experience.

I think it would come as no surprise that I have run the full gamut of emotions when trying to come to terms with the losses in my life. Death as a result of old age affects you much differently than death caused by a freak health incident or suicide. It is not that one type of death has been heavier than another, it is just that I have carried the load a little differently with each. And yes, I have had to leave a lot of pebbles at the cross over regrets with the losses in my life. I have also packed a lot more weights than I would like to admit when I cannot seem to leave those pebbles well enough alone.

But that is the thing about grief. It is not linear. It ebbs and flows. It softens and then it stabs. You come to terms with it, and then you question everything about it – including if you could have changed the end result.

The reality, though, is that death knocks on all of our doors. That is why I made it a point to include the last blog post regarding my encounter with Buster in the park. That chance conversation made me realize how important it is for each of us to reflect on what we want to be remembered/cherished for after we leave this Earth. My lost loved ones have left behind beautiful legacies I now carry with me. I aim to do the same.

What I hope these blog posts conveyed above all else is that grief and love can coexist. One does not have to replace the other when we lose our loved ones or when the world breaks our heart. And even though love is a choice and loss is a guarantee, I hope today and every day forward we choose love.

Because if love is guiding all we do, then what we are doing on Earth becomes a lot more meaningful.

Scan to View Images

EPILOGUE

Well friends, we made it to the end of our quest. But before I let you go, I want to challenge your way of thinking one last time.

At the beginning of this book, I informed you we were going to explore a question throughout the text together. I ask you to now flip back to the cover of the book to remind yourself of that question. And as you stare at the title, I want you to make note of the punctuation.

Then I want you to flip to the table of contents. As you examine the titles of each part of the book, what stands out to you? What word do you notice referenced multiple times?

When you have your answers to these questions, return here to the epilogue for some final thoughts to ponder.

———

What I hope you took note of in the title is that it is filled with commas and a question mark. That is because there used to not be a day that passed in which I did not ask the question, "What on Earth am I doing?" But now, there is not a day that passes I do not instead ask, "What, on Earth, am I doing?"

Do you see the difference?

The first iteration of the question is filled with doubt. Uncertainty. A lack of belief in oneself. The second, however, is filled with curiosity. Intrigue. The conviction to want to make a difference.

I made it a point to not emphasize the power commas can have when I first introduced this question at the beginning of the book. I intentionally did that because before all of the adventures, life lessons, loss, heartbreak, and renewed faith and hope I have experienced in my life and shared with you, I was a victim of asking the first iteration of the question far too much. But as I have journeyed through life and weathered the storms, I have come to understand the power behind asking the second question instead.

You see, life's commas function much in the same way as grammar's commas. They offer a time to pause, reflect, catch our breath, and then continue on. Asking ourselves the second question gives us time to really ponder what we want to do on this Earth before our time is up.

And speaking of that, what word was it that you noticed multiple times on the table of contents? Hopefully, your answer is "living." Each part of the book is accordingly titled with this word because in all the good and bad, that is what I choose to continue to do. To live life one day to the next because we are never promised tomorrow.

So friends, here is where I am going to implore you to ask yourselves the question one final time, "What, on Earth, am I doing?"

Here is what I hope you are doing on Earth:

- Living your most abandoned life
- Planning one adventure after another
- Prioritizing "Only Jesus"
- Laughing when you encounter life's misadventures
- Chasing after your purpose, but not being consumed by trying to discover it
- Choosing to love great instead of just good enough
- Striving to leave others better than you found them

I hope you are choosing to do all of these things on Earth, so that when you get to the end of your time, and someone asks you what, on Earth, you did, you can undoubtedly answer:

"I chose to actively live, instead of patiently die."

ACKNOWLEDGEMENTS

While there still may be days I question what on Earth it is that I am here to do, one thing I know for certain is that I am here to show gratitude.

First and foremost, this book would not be a reality without the never-ending love and support of my parents, Tom and Chellee Price.

My mom was the first reader of this work and also the one willing to stay up with me into the wee hours of the night. Her insight was invaluable in offering suggestions as I edited my manuscript and in helping me whittle down what pictures to include with my blogs. Additionally, the faith she instilled in me at a young age will forever be the guiding force of my life and is such an important component of this book.

My dad deserves a hearty thank you for gifting me with his sense of humor and tireless work ethic. Over the years, he has taught me the importance of always keeping a positive attitude and leading with a servant heart; two things he does better than anyone I know. I am most grateful for the banks he is to my wildly flowing river.

I want to extend an equally huge thank you to my sister Chandler. She truly is my other half and the person I can always confide in, especially when the adventures I plan are too harrowing to share with our parents. Her constant support has sustained me on the mountaintops and in the valleys. I could not be more blessed to do this life with her.

Thank you to my grandma, Mickey, who instilled in me a love for reading from a young age. It is this exposure that ignited the passion within me to become a writer myself. Minds do not come sharper nor hearts more golden than hers.

A sincere thank you goes out to my editor, Cheryl Wilde. Her technicality and attention to detail are second to none and helped me strengthen my work while allowing me to maintain my voice and message throughout. The hours we spent talking on the phone and communicating ideas through email will remain some of my favorite memories of bringing this book to life.

Next, I would be remiss if I did not thank my village of friends and family who never fail to support me in all I do. There are too many to list here in fear of leaving someone out. Each and every one of them have touched my heart in more ways than one and have helped me along my journey of discovering what on Earth it is I am here to do. They have also helped me carry bags with a lot of weights in them.

I further want to thank those who provided a roof over my head or a bed to sleep in during my domestic and international travels. Their hospitality enriched my experiences described within this book.

In memory, I would like to thank those no longer present with me on this Earth, but who will forever occupy a special place in my heart. I am convinced I have the most equipped guardian angels who protect me every day. There have been a couple close calls on a few of my adventures, so I thank them for ultimately keeping me safe so I could compose this publication.

Lastly, I would like to thank God above all else. Without Him, I would be aimlessly wondering about this Earth. His love and mercy never fail, and I for one am incredibly grateful for His willingness to leave the ninety-nine to find the lost one. He has rescued me more times than I deserve.

LETTER FROM THE AUTHOR

Dear Friends,

I have always loved the quote by Gloria Steinem that states, "Writing is the only thing that, when I do it, I don't feel like I should be doing something else."

There are a lot of other activities I could have chosen to do over the last nine years, but none would have been as meaningful as the time I spent writing the blogs that ultimately culminated in producing this book.

It was about two years ago that the idea of this book came to me. I was sitting in my apartment in Columbia, Missouri, reflecting back on how much I missed connecting with others through blogging. But rather than write a blog about that, I thought about how fun it would be to coalesce all of my previous blogs into one book. I decided, though, I wanted to go one step further and also add commentary that reflected a current assessment of my past experiences.

The greatest gift of crafting this book was that it provided me the opportunity to go back and reread about the adventures, struggles, heartbreak, and lessons learned that have shaped me into the person I am today. I had to laugh as I combed through some of the old blogs and could explicitly see where some of my previous thoughts and beliefs have changed with time and perspective. For example, at the time I wrote most of the blogs, I had not yet become an aunt. As I read about my less than thrilled mindset whenever I had to interact with kids, I had to laugh as my niece and nephew now mean the absolute world to me. And while the idea of having kids of my own has not necessarily grown on me, loving and embracing those of others most definitely has.

I think if anything, that is the beauty of this book. It is that even I recognize that the me who wrote these blogs is not the same person in many ways because life demands that we constantly grow and evolve. In the last decade of my life, I have lived in different states and countries and each place has afforded me wonderful memories, lessons, and lifelong friends I could not imagine my life without.

I am also positive the college freshman who started blogging in 2015 about struggling to find purpose or a dedicated career path could never have fathomed she would have five different jobs by the time she was 27. But I have learned that it is ok if careers reach their expiry dates too because that is how we remain fresh in pursuing our purpose. I recognize that much like a seed, I have to get out of a familiar package in order to grow, so I tend to pursue opportunities where I have a chance to do that. This mindset has enabled me to surround myself with people that make me think bigger, work harder, and test the limits of what I ever thought was possible. Who knows, one day I might just become that cognitive neuroscientist.

I will admit too that I struggled at first about how vulnerable I wanted to be in this book or what blogs I might want to leave out because they are a bit more personal. Arguably, the blogs that tug the most on my heartstrings are my blogs about those I have lost. Those are the times I have been brought to my knees; the traumas that have altered me as a person. But they are also the blogs that have led me to embracing the beauty of acceptance. And that has been acceptance for both myself and for others. If you recall in my blog about my papa, I mention how he loved my cow-splatter freckles and crooked smile. That crooked smile is the result of an unknown virus that afflicted me at the age of two and has resulted in residual paralysis in my left arm and face. I briefly share that insight into my childhood with you now to illustrate that acceptance has been a lifelong journey for me, and that I have learned that what truly matters most in life is displaying resiliency in the face of our hardships.

Thus, I ultimately decided that all blogs were going to make the cut because this book would not be a true manifestation of myself if they were not included. This resulted in me sharing my greatest insecurities with my readers, i.e. the thoughts that keep me up at night. Or in other words, the pebbles I have a hard time leaving undisturbed. But I figured if I could share my personal struggles in the hope it could help others, then maybe we could all learn to start carrying lighter loads. After all, part of what we should be doing on this Earth is figuring out how to help walk each other home.

And speaking of home, I must confess I did not ask for permission to include the blogs that featured my family and friends. So, to that end, I will just have to beg their forgiveness. But it is like the saying goes, "Life takes you to unexpected places, love brings you home." The people in this book are my home, so they deserve to be featured in it.

This manuscript truly is a compilation of all the adventures, people, places, and lessons I hold dearly within my heart. While it may have been a decade in the making, it represents a lifetime of memories captured in print.